Dragged Aboard

Dragged Aboard

A Cruising Guide for the Reluctant Mate

Don Casey

Illustrations by Don Almquist

W. W. NORTON & COMPANY
NEW YORK LONDON

For information about permission to reproduce selections from this book,
write to Permissions, W. W. Norton & Company, Inc., 500 Fifth Avenue,
New York, NY 10110.

The text of this book is composed in Minion
with the display set in Minion Semibold
Book design and composition by Faith Hague Book Design
Manufacturing by Haddon Craftsmen
Illustrations by Don Almquist

Library of Congress Cataloging-in-Publication Data
Casey, Don
        Dragged aboard: a cruising guide for the reluctant mate / Don Casey;
with illustrations by Don Almquist.
            p.   cm.
        Includes index.
        1. Sailboat Living. 2. Family recreation. I. Title.
        GV811.65.C37   1998
        797.1—dc21   97-49571
                                                                              CIP

ISBN 0-393-04653-2

W. W. Norton & Company, Inc., 500 Fifth Avenue, New York, N.Y. 10110
        http://www.wwnorton.com
W. W. Norton & Company Ltd., 10 Coptic Street, London WC1A 1PU

1 2 3 4 5 6 7 8 9 0

A fire-fly flitted by:
"Look!" I almost said,—
But I was alone.

—Taigi

This book is lovingly dedicated to Olga,
without whom I also am alone.

Contents

Introduction

WHEN I FIRST ENCOUNTERED THE CONCEPT OF CRUISING, IN A *NATIONAL Geographic* article about teenage sailor Robin Lee Graham, it was a revelation, a religious experience. I was in my final year of college when suddenly confronted with a 16-year-old boy traveling in a 24-foot sailboat to the most exotic places on the globe. Graham's adventure and lifestyle made my imminent embarkation on a 40-year climb up the corporate ladder seem—awful.

I graduated, found employment in a coastal city, bought a sailboat, and was single-mindedly preparing myself to follow in Graham's wake when I was visited by a second religious experience. Two years after we were married, Olga and I left families, jobs, and possessions behind and set off on a six-month "trial cruise."

Almost from the start the disparity in our perspectives was obvious. I was always anxious for our next departure; Olga's joy came when we arrived. My favorite anchorages were those bereft of other boats; Olga saw empty harbors as . . . well . . . empty. I didn't give much thought to bedding, crow's-feet, or the next meal. Olga hated clammy sheets, considered sun the enemy, and wasn't surprised at my rare concern for meals since that also was how often I prepared them. Because cruising was my dream, I simply overlooked even obvious shortcomings. Olga, on the other hand, suffered no delusion that foot pumps and windscoops were the equal of hot showers and air conditioning.

This last truth might have ultimately defined cruising for her had we not stayed out long enough to get extraordinarily healthy, discover a wider world, make wonderful friends, and get used to spending our time together. That every single hour belonged to us was a level of luxury neither had imagined, and when our time ran out we were equally reluctant to return to the demands of life ashore.

I didn't really have to drag Olga aboard for that first cruise, but she invariably described it as something *I* wanted to do. My efforts to give her a glimpse of the Nirvana I imagined failed, and had my own determination faltered, Olga would have been just as happy—happier maybe. So most of the preparation fell to me, which seemed only fair, and when we finally cast off, Olga was more passenger than partner.

It didn't take long on that first trip to discover that we were not unusual. It was the rare couple who began their cruise with equal enthusiasm. More often half of the twosome started out ambivalent at best, disconsolate at worst. Yet, as with us, the realities of cruising soon superseded predeparture notions. Those most resistant at the start often were the ones having the best time—like discovering a chest pain was just last night's burrito.

If your partner dreams of sailing away and you are—how should I put this?—cool to the idea, this book was written just for you. You won't find a single word about hull design or sail inventory or bilge pump configurations—the usual fare of cruising books. The focus here is solidly on living, on minimizing the limitations and maximizing the rewards of traveling under sail. It is a book about staying comfortable and healthy in an unfamiliar environment, about solving the litany of domestic challenges boats present, about what you should take along and what has to stay behind. In short, it is about making the transition from life ashore to life aboard a cruising boat. It is tempting to call it a survival guide, but cruising presents far too many opportunities for enjoyment to set such a limiting objective.

Wherever cruisers gather, there are almost always two conversations going on simultaneously. One is about anchors and sails and diesel engines, the other about health and laundry and calling home. In my early years of cruising I was part of the anchor group, but a dozen or so years ago I switched. There was more heat than light in the anchor and sail discussions because these subjects are covered in mind-numbing detail in virtually every book about cruising, but the health and laundry discussions were often peppered with original ideas for improving life aboard. They regularly yielded ingenious solutions to the very deficiencies Olga found most off-putting (and I had tried hardest to ignore). Even when they didn't provide answers, they revealed essential questions. Those cockpit discussions are the genesis of this book.

I have already admitted to a love of cruising, and for that I make no apology, but my blinders blew away years ago. Here, without filters or flattering light, you'll find a comprehensive look at the cruising lifestyle, the bitter with the sweet. I'm not out to convert you any more than I want to convince you that, say, your favorite color should be green, although I'm not above pointing out the green when it enhances the palette.

And let's clear the air on the gender issue. Men have been going to sea—mostly with other men—for at least 3,500 years. Little boys are raised on the adventures of Sinbad, Blackbeard, Cook, Bligh, Ahab, and Huck and Jim, so it shouldn't be surprising that men are more susceptible to the lure of cruising. When only half of a twosome has cruising fever, odds are it's the man. This alone is the basis for all gender assumptions this book contains.

Cruisers have long been a literate lot, committing experience and opinion to print, but when I tried early on to get Olga to read the "best" of the cruising books, they just made her eyes glaze over. If they harbored information she would have found helpful, it was well shielded by a preponderance of text about topics in which she had zero interest. In the two decades since, cruising books haven't much changed, but I have, so I decided to write the book I wish I could have handed to Olga years ago. This is it. I am happy to report that not only did Olga read it cover to cover without nodding off, she gives it a glowing review.

It is my fondest hope that you also will find this effort both arresting and informative. If you are apprehensive about cruising, perhaps this book will allay some of your fears. If you are just disinterested, maybe you haven't considered all the possibilities. At the very least the body of knowledge in these pages can make a cruise, even a reluctant one, considerably easier. As to whether it will also cause a fundamental shift in your enthusiasm, maybe not. But that's OK, because happily, precruise conceptions don't seem to have much correlation to whether one ultimately loves the cruising life or hates it. The proof, as they say, is in the pudding.

1

What Is Cruising Really Like?

CRUISING—TRAVELING THE WORLD'S WATERWAYS IN YOUR OWN VESSEL— is not new. The wealthy have been doing it for a couple of centuries, but it didn't become a viable option for the rest of us, aside from a few hardy types, until boatbuilders embraced fiberglass in the 1960s. Suddenly, thanks to fiberglass construction, boats large enough to include living accommodations became affordable, both to purchase and to maintain.

To those with sufficient imagination, a boat with overnight accommodations is much more than just a floating second home. It is a magic carpet, a gold pass to the world beyond the horizon. Point the bow, catch the wind, and you and your home can be transported—free of charge—to virtually any place on the globe.

That is the fantasy. The reality is that boats are typically cramped, damp, and hot or cold. They demand unending maintenance, constant vigilance, and their rolling and bucking can be downright nauseating.

So why even consider cruising? Why not just say no? Maybe you have a comfortable home, a job you like. You are surrounded by friends and family. What could cruising possibly offer that would lead you to leave all this behind and sail off into the fog of the unknown? That is the question, isn't it?

The catch is that you have to go to know. But almost everyone who does go cruising reaches the same conclusion: the rewards far outweigh the sacrifices. Let me share with you, as even-handedly as I can, some of the attractions of the cruising life, and a few of its limitations. But first, a word of caution to all who are considering their first cruise.

Starting Slow

The cruising literature is full of stories of people with little or no experience who leave their home dock and put straight to sea, headed for a destination 1,000 or more miles distant. It is instructive (and reassuring) that they invariably arrive, sometimes a bit wide-eyed, but otherwise unharmed by their overreach.

Such misguided souls typically have allotted a set amount of time to their cruise—six months, perhaps a year—and if they're going to visit all the places on their *itinerary,* they've got to get going. This initial mind-set is common and not very surprising. After all, the year or two prior to a cruise is almost always dominated by a rigid plan, requiring certain things to happen by specific dates if the cruise is to get off on time. Not to mention that our lives ashore in general are structured around dates, times, and commitments.

It's hard to suddenly turn off the switch on this mind-set, but cruising to a schedule is sheer folly. And trying to "make miles" at the start risks tarnishing or even derailing the cruise entirely, especially if anyone is aboard reluctantly.

It is essential to understand that a cruise is underway as soon as the mooring pendant is dropped or the last dockline comes aboard. *You are not going somewhere; you're already there.* I'm not suggesting limited horizons—sail to Tierra del Fuego if you want to—but on Day One find a not-too-distant cove or a quiet creek and put the anchor down for a day or two. Let your body adjust to the rhythm of the boat, your mind to the emancipation of cruising.

Master of Your Own Time

Emancipation. A good word to describe one of cruising's strongest attractions. Life ashore has a tendency to enslave. No matter how late you got to bed the night before, the alarm goes off at 6 A.M. The last train leaves the station at 7:42. A rush on the Grunwald account means lunch at the desk—if at all. Home at 7, dinner at 8. There's nothing on the tube, but you watch it anyway, too spent to do anything else. Read? Not after 10 hours of Grunwald. Floss. Gargle. The evening wardrobe crisis. Then fall into bed.

It is true that cruising has its own form of bondage, but not the mind-numbing sort of life ashore. Every day is different. Scheduled activities are soon limited to a single item: "Let's go diving today." "Want to see what they have in the market?" "Let me change the oil in the engine, then we'll kick back." The rest of the day unfolds naturally:

The crew from *Windsong* comes by for a chat and to drop off a recipe. An impromptu volleyball game starts up on the beach. A midday rain shower calls the game—and cools the air. You read 100 pages of *Shipping News,* take a short nap, make fresh lemonade.

The couple off *Quixote* come by to invite you for paella—late. You read 50 more pages, take a refreshing dip, wash your hair, rinse it with buckets of soft rainwater from the dinghy. Maybe you'll wear your new Androsia.

Fresh seafood makes the paella great. *Cool Change* is also at the party, Robyn with her guitar. When she begins to sing, halyards ching in the darkness as other cruisers in the anchorage come on deck to listen. A kerosene lantern flickering in the night breeze bathes the cockpit gathering with bronze light. At the end of a pointing finger a satellite rushes across the night sky; at the end of a silver ribbon a full moon rises above the horizon. It is 3 A.M. before everyone slips quietly away and glides home.

Six o'clock comes and goes. Sunlight finally overcomes eyelids at 10:30. Brunch at 11.

"Want to go diving today?"

The Rebirth of Conviviality

Answer this question honestly: How many friends (or potential friends) have you let drift away because you didn't have time for them? Or how many good friends do you have whom you haven't seen in the last six months?

Olga and I feel guilty about the way we neglect our friends. If your calls to friends often start with "Where has time gone?" or "I meant to call you sooner," you know what I'm talking about. We almost never initiate new friendships ashore and usually brush off overtures because we don't have time for the friends we already have. It's sad, but it's the truth.

Community is a central tenet of the cruising life. Cruisers have time for friendship; it doesn't take a back seat to job responsibilities or housework. New friends are an everyday occurrence. Take your morning coffee in the cockpit and someone is likely to stop by and share it with you. Lunch may be a spontaneous potluck on the beach with everyone from the anchorage. Shared dinners are a nearly nightly event—if you want them to be.

You will establish more lifelong friendships in six months of cruising than in six years ashore. Why? Because of the flux of the cruising community.

You hit it off with Bill and Robyn on *Cool Change,* and for the next 10 days you are inseparable—diving together, sharing a car to visit an inland waterfall, alternating boats for dinner. Then they sail south and you sail east.

Sounds horrible? You hate good-byes? I didn't say anything about goodbye. Here's how it goes. At your next port you meet Nigel and Sally on *Lord Nelson.* You picnic together, swap paperbacks, discuss the condition of the world late into the night. Nigel announces shared dinners with a horn crafted from a huge pink conch shell. Inevitably *Lord Nelson* moves on, slipping away one day before sunup to reach her next destination in daylight. When you come on deck that morning, the conch horn you so admired is nestled carefully in the aft corner of your cockpit.

That same day *Puff* sails in on a dying breeze, carrying Jim, Janice, and 7-year-old Joshua aboard. And so on. And so on. And so on.

Then the day comes when you arrive at a crowded anchorage. "Look, isn't that *Cool Change*?" *Lord Nelson* is there too. And *Puff.* The good times flow.

In the cruising community, nearby friends are seen daily. For those no longer nearby, you simply look forward to the day when your paths again converge, knowing that it will be a particularly happy day.

Friendships you make cruising continue long after the cruise is over—something concrete and precious you bring back with you. But won't all these new friends just make matters worse when you get back? No. Cruisers accept long absences as the norm, which only make get-togethers that much better.

Expect to add at least a couple of your cruising friends to your inner circle ashore, but also expect to come back with a new social perspective that will lead you to restructure your life to allow more time for friends. Of the friends that keep cruising or come ashore far away, some will stop by whenever they are "in the neighborhood," or you will visit them under similar circumstances, and these reunions will be like crossing paths afloat—wonderful, and comfortable in a way you probably have to experience to understand. Others you will keep up with only through their annual newsletter to their scattered cadre of friends. And some you will lose track of altogether—like your best friend in 9th grade—but you will never lose the memories. When you dust that conch horn on a gray winter day, your smile will cut the chill.

Meeting the World

Nigel and Sally are from England. Sally always serves dinner on china, but none of the pieces match. "That'd be boring, wouldn't it, love?" she says. She makes a chicken curry that changes your opinion about curries forever. Nigel was stationed in Belfast when he served in the British Army, and one evening he gives a firsthand account that for the first time makes the "Troubles" in Northern Ireland real and comprehendible.

Quixote is from Spain. Carlos voices strong views on everything. "Three Spaniards, four opinions," he laughs. Mercedes always looks like she is in a fashion shoot. She wonders how dangerous it might be to visit America. You are surprised to learn that Spain has cities on the African side of the Mediterranean.

If your cruise takes you far from home, particularly to foreign cruising grounds such as the Bahamas, Caribbean, Mexico, or Pacific islands, you will share anchorages with cruisers from all over the world. In light of how homogenous—even parochial—most neighborhoods are, finding yourself in a "world" community is exciting, fun, and often enlightening.

Consider a few of the cruising friends Olga and I have. They are from Florida, Texas, California, New York, Washington, Maine, and Chimney Rock, Colorado. They are also from France, Germany, England, Spain, Switzerland, Canada, and South Africa. They range from well below the poverty line to multimillionaires. There are several types of engineers, a nurse, a famous singer, several writers, a naval architect, the owner of a manufacturing company, assorted teachers, a waitress, a contractor, a boat painter, a commercial pilot, a speculator in gemstones, a colonel, a farmer, an ocean racer, and a retired bank president.

A sundowner or a beach party with some of this group is always informative. We might get tips on snow skiing, insight on the strife in South Africa, learn how to build a house, how to fly an airplane, what makes an emerald valuable, why American farmers are going broke, what it's like to cross an ocean alone, or how to convince a bank to loan us money.

A few cruisers fly the so-called "world flag." It is appropriate. There are no borders in the cruising community, no immigrants, no aliens. Everyone, no matter what country issued their passport or what language they speak, is dedicated to the same principles: seeing, doing, learning, enjoying.

Seeing the World

The success of a cruise should never be measured in miles. When time is short, a cruise is likely to be more successful—in terms of enjoyment—if distances are modest. Even with more time available, far-off destinations are not essential. But because your accommodations are traveling with you, cruising is a linear activity—like walking. When you move, it is only natural that your destination will be somewhere "new." Even if each of these "steps" is small, put enough of them together and you find yourself far from your departure point. Average only 20 miles each day and a 4-year cruise can take you right around the globe.

How hard is it to imagine someplace you'd like to see? Do you think those Bahamas ads on television are trick photography, shot through special filters to give the water that incredible color? Think again. There are no adjectives sufficiently rhapsodic to describe the water colors. As you cruise through this island country you are afloat in a 700-mile-long aquarium. Look over the side on a still day and you see kaleidoscopic fish parading through red and purple corals *a hundred feet down.*

In Trinidad you sit quietly on the veranda of the old plantation home of the Asa Wright Nature Centre and study dozens of exotic birds perched like Christmas ornaments in the bushes just beyond the railing, while iridescent hummingbirds the size of bumblebees hover at arm's length and study you. The following week is Carnival. You join a band and—along with the entire population of Port of Spain—"chip" through the streets in the pulsating air behind a tractor-trailer load of maxed-out loudspeakers, dancing until the sun comes up over the Savanna.

You didn't know what a *mola* was until you arrived in the Lalique waters of the Kuna Yala off the north coast of Panama. Then for three weeks the perfect *mola* became the Holy Grail as you sailed from island to island in your quest. *Molas* are exquisite reverse-appliquéd and embroidered cloth panels that are traditionally part of the blouses worn by the Kuna Indians, but the best ones are not out of place as framed art. A smiling Kuna girl who calls herself Felipa turns two *molas* into beautiful accent pillows for the main salon.

Maybe yours is a Pacific cruise. Along the Baja coast you dine on fresh lobster five nights in a row, finally giving your arteries a break with grilled dorado. In the Galápagos you read Darwin's *Voyage of the* Beagle aloud as you visit islands virtually unchanged since his 1835 visit. In the Marquesas you take up wearing the eminently sensible and stunningly beautiful Polynesian sarong. Tourists you meet in Papeete astonish you with the cost of their one-week visit—more than you've spent in over three months.

This exercise is endless. Tied up among pastel boats with melodious names, your overnight stop in a picturesque fishing port in Portugal is stretched by hospitality into more than a month. Or ancient Doric columns tower over a whitewashed village clinging to land as steep as a cow's face as you sip Greek wine in a quayside cafe. Or after the quiet of flower-lined canals and the quaintness of lock-keepers who collect their modest fee in a dangled wooden shoe, you tie up in Paris with the south rose window of Notre Dame overhead.

Paris notwithstanding, maybe you don't want to see the world just from its shores. I couldn't agree with you more. For coastal cruising in America, many cruisers find good use for bicycles or small mopeds. For more distant inland destinations, rental cars are available. Share the car with another cruising couple and you'll double the fun and halve the cost. Europe has a system of trains that go everywhere, all the time, on time, and inexpensively. In Mexico you will be on the bus, cheap and an adventure all its own. Every place has some transportation system residents use; you can use it, too.

We know so little about the world beyond our normal circle, and experiencing as much of it as we can is as good a reason as any for setting off on a cruise. Pick a destination you would like to visit, a distant event you would like to attend, and make that the focus of your planning. It will make a cruise less like dropping out and more like dropping in.

Dark Skies

"What about storms?"

That's the first question almost everyone new to cruising asks, so let's get right to it. Storms happen. Weather systems circle the globe, and they pass over where you are, whether mid-Kansas or mid-Atlantic. But on a typical cruise—where offshore passages, if any, are measured in days rather than weeks—the prudent skipper can (and should) avoid getting caught out in a major storm system. This doesn't include local thunderstorms, which can boil up unexpectedly out of a peacock-blue sky.

You have been enjoying a perfect day of sailing, headed from the Biminis across the Little Bahama Bank. The breeze has been far enough to the south to allow the bow to point directly at your destination. The wind has strengthened with the shortening morning shadows. At the bow a bubbly champagne party replaces the earlier chuckle. For the last two hours you have been sitting forward of the bow wave, staring into the bottle-clear water to watch starfish the color of paprika and sea fans like lavender lace glide beneath the boat.

The shadow gets your attention first, and when you look up, you are alarmed at the color of the sky ahead. Aft you find the captain wary, but reluctant to give up the good breeze unnecessarily. He waits too long. The first gust slams into the spread of sail like a divine fist, knocking the boat nearly flat in the water. You take the wheel while he tries to take sail off. The wind shrieks. The captain shouts. Sails clap like gunfire. The boat staggers. The sea smokes. Waves explode into a hail of spray. Pandemonium reigns.

In 10 minutes it's over. The roll of the boat slows like the pendulum of a run-down clock, then stops altogether as straight-down rain peens the sea flat. You desert the wheel and go below to towel off, stopping in mid-rub to contemplate the library-like serenity of the cabin. Varnished mahogany gleams reassuringly. Nothing is out of place, your own wet footprints the only sign of the tumult.

An hour later the bow is again slicing the sea into white curls as you sail toward a blue horizon.

Thunderstorms almost never give a well-found and wisely handled cruising boat more than a jostle and a wash, but finding yourself on a boat in the middle of a particularly boisterous boomer can still be frightening. This is a good time for perspective. Images of solidly anchored homes reduced to rubble by wind, flood, mud, and tremor parade regularly across the evening news. By comparison, a cruising boat is virtually immune to weather. A well-built boat is incredibly tough: the roof isn't going to blow off, the windows won't blow in, and 40 days of rain won't even wet the rug.

Water

You have found paradise, or at least a slice of it. The cove is large enough for 30 boats, but only 3 are in it. Palms lean out over a powder sand beach in post-card perfection. Like pink and purple fireworks, bright blooms of hibiscus and bougainvillea explode among the greenery behind the beach. Bands of gambling snapper cruise through every evening, anxious to try their luck at removing the bait from your hook. Lobster are packed so thick into the reef astern that it resembles a Moscow housing block. Conch are holding a convention in the shallows.

But this morning you have checked, measured, and calculated. Your water supply is running uncomfortably low; you can stay maybe one more day. Then, in one of the ironies of cruising, the distant rumble of thunder lifts your spirits. The sky darkens to the south. "Here," you entreat. "Come here."

Wham! The thunderstorm roars over the cove like a locomotive. The boat heels, spins, and rushes backward until both anchor lines thrum straight. You silently acknowledge the captain's wisdom in setting two anchors and diving on them to make sure they were buried. Like the boomer that caught you on the Bank, the wind in this thunderstorm lasts only minutes, then the rain falls in buckets. The hose from your catchment awning gurgles, then roars, pouring gallon after gallon into your tanks until the fill line bubbles up like a playground fountain. The rain continues, and you fill jugs, buckets, pots—anything that will hold water. Still it rains. You take a bar of soap and a bottle of shampoo to the foredeck and stand naked under the downpour until every pore is slaked. The laundry soon joins you on deck. By the time the

trailing edge of the storm drags sunlight back across the cove, rigging and life-lines are festooned with clean clothes, towels, and bed linens.

This is one of cruising's best moments. Rain-filled water tanks provide a sense of well-being, a sense of found wealth that cannot be explained. It is as though you have been found worthy, and God has paid your tab for another 30 days. It makes the point that while thunderstorms are unavoidable, they aren't malicious. You may never come to enjoy these little tantrums of nature, but you are certain to welcome this benefit of their passage.

Limited fresh water is one of the discomforts of cruising. Ashore you can turn the tap and clear, safe (?) water will run out until you turn it off again. The average American uses *65 gallons of water a day*. The total tank capacity in a cruising boat crewed by two is unlikely to much exceed 130 gallons—a one-day supply.

Of course no cruiser uses 65 gallons a day. Most limit freshwater consumption to about 1 gallon per person per day. How? By substituting unlimited seawater whenever possible. This isn't particularly inconvenient for deck-washing, dishwashing, or flushing the toilet, but anyone who tells you she or he doesn't miss long, lingering showers is lying. Strategies for dealing with this limitation are detailed later, but none is as impossibly luxurious as city water.

On the other hand, a growing segment of our population distrusts tap water for drinking. Is there any purer source of water than rain? Municipalities are also increasingly unable to meet the demand of our injudicious water usage. Going cruising can stop you from being part of the problem and make you part of the solution. Cruising opens your eyes to conservation in a way that lasts longer than just the time you are off the grid.

Unplugged

The other two boats in your cove are *Figaro* and *Sandpiper*. Aboard *Figaro* Linda uses an electric range, has a microwave oven in the galley, brews coffee in an electric pot. Vents along the front of the settee pour refrigerated air into the main salon. It feels wonderful. On this hot night, putting up with the rumble and vibration of the diesel generator seems to you a small price to pay for such luxury. *Does the generator run all the time?* "Except when *Figaro* is plugged in at a dock," Dan tells you.

Rowing home you do the math. Just the fuel cost is more than $500 a month. "Lots of engine hours," your partner comments. "Add a couple of hundred a month in rebuild cost." Yet another drawback becomes obvious when a wind shift puts *Figaro* upwind, and the tranquillity of your little paradise is sullied by the splash of exhaust and the odor of diesel fumes.

Paul is alone aboard his birdlike trimaran. He serves the best cup of coffee you've ever tasted, grinding the beans in a hand-cranked mill and brewing the coffee by pouring boiling water through the grounds. There is nothing electric in *Sandpiper*'s galley except a single fluorescent light. His stereo is a Walkman. Except for a couple of cabin lights, only his running lights and his radio are connected to the ship's battery. His motor is an outboard, so he runs a tiny gasoline generator one or twice a week to keep his single battery up.

The electrical system aboard most cruising boats is somewhere between these two extremes. Here is the key fact: unless you're going from marina to marina (bring along a bag full of cash), all the electricity you use you have to generate yourself. That means for cruisers without *Figaro*'s apparent means, most "modern conveniences" are not going on the cruise with you. Getting along without an electric can opener is not much of a sacrifice, but who wants to go back to handwashing clothes?

Allow me a small digression. Doing without a washer (and dryer) is not as big a step back as it seems. In the first place, if you're going to the usual cruising destinations, you won't be wearing a lot of clothes. And there are laundromats all over the world. If your shoreside wardrobe includes many "delicates," you may actually be doing more handwashing ashore than you will do on the boat. (Don't take delicates.)

Heating appliances draw gobs of power and are particularly incompatible with the limited electrical capacity of most boats. You may miss the automatic coffeemaker and the toaster, but the iron, curlers, and hair dryer—like the alarm clock—tend to lose their importance when you're cruising. Most cruisers do fine without on-demand hot water, but if you need it, there are nonelectrical solutions.

Your boat is sure to have power for running lights, radios, and other electronics, but make sure it also has enough additional power for comfortable cabin lighting. Most cruisers also value a CD player. And on the water, a couple of good cabin fans can be nearly as effective as air conditioning. Beyond that, you won't miss the rest of the stuff plugged into your outlets at home—with one exception.

Cold Truth

It is late at night and you decide to slip out to the galley for a snack—maybe a mound of leftover shrimp salad on a bed of cold lettuce. You open the refrigerator door, and the light spills out. The salad is right in front. You open the crisper drawer for the lettuce. On the top shelf is that bottle of nice Chablis. You find a package of crisp breadsticks tucked into the door of the freezer.

What can we tell from this scene? That either you're dreaming or you're still at home. Maybe Linda over on *Figaro* has a regular refrigerator with a crisper, glass shelves, and a light, but unless you are prepared to take on the expense and relentlessness of a constant-running generator, your onboard refrigerator is more likely to resemble a picnic cooler—both in size and configuration. That's OK; it will still keep the shrimp salad cold, and the lettuce if you have room.

The fact is that in America we refrigerate a lot of foods that don't require it. Away from America you find fewer refrigerated items for sale. If *Figaro* is more than a week or two from the last supermarket, it is a certainty that everything in Linda's cavernous fridge that *needs refrigeration* will fit on less than half a shelf. Ignoring the freezer compartment, which is another issue, this means that Linda's house-size refrigerator offers no benefit beyond familiarity.

Even a modest refrigerator takes a lot of power, which generally translates into running the engine daily. Some don't seem to mind; others find listening to the engine *every day* for an hour or two (sometimes more) intolerable. Aside from the noise, there is the fuel cost (nominal) and the wear and tear on the engine (substantial—diesels suffer from running under a light load). Perhaps worse is the obligation; you have to be aboard at about the same time every day. That complicates plans as simple as an overnight excursion aboard another boat, and it is a significant deterrent to inland tours and trips home.

Some eventually conclude that the demands and complexity of refrigeration detract too much from the cruising experience and choose to cruise without it. For those few things aboard that need to be refrigerated, adding a fresh block of ice to an insulated cooler twice a week can suffice, but ice isn't always available, it isn't always cheap, and chasing it down and getting it back to the boat soon get tiring.

Most people setting off on a first cruise cannot imagine doing without refrigeration. The gastronomic compromises required by its absence seem unacceptable. Hot days without cool drinks are unthinkable. If you are among this majority, here is a truism that will serve you well: *smaller is always better.* Limiting the size of your refrigerator to the absolute minimum vastly improves the likelihood that it will prove to be convenience rather than tyranny. You'll find help with the refrigeration dilemma in later pages.

Space

The girl from the red boat is tossing duffel bags into *Figaro*'s launch. She is blond, tan, lithe. Her husband, boyfriend, or whatever—you're not sure—is prudently watching from the beach. Linda has agreed to deliver the girl up-island to where she can catch a plane for home. When the bags are loaded, she stands for a moment on her boat, runs her fingers absently over the varnish of a handrail, then stiffens and steps into the launch. Linda shoves the throttle forward, and the space between the girl and the red boat seems to stretch like taffy. You wait for it to snap, feeling sad and slightly apprehensive.

Robyn's distinctive laughter intrudes and makes you look toward *Cool Change,* once again anchored nearby, but you don't see anyone aboard. You hear Robyn again, follow the sound, and find their red inflatable dinghy bouncing across the harbor in puffs of spray. They pass *Cool Change* in a sweeping arc and glide to a stop a foot from your boat.

Robyn is soaked. Her blouse is plastered to her body, and her hair hangs straight down on either side of her face. She is flushed and still laughing. Bill, in contrast, is relatively dry, and his ears are joined by a crescent grin. He moves forward in the dinghy and rummages around in a canvas bag at Robyn's feet, producing a purple orb so large it takes you a second to realize it is an eggplant. "And . . . ," he says, and extracts an equally magnificent pineapple from the bag. "All in all a successful shore raid. Eggplant parmigiana at 6:30. A black tie affair."

Bill and Robyn work together in *Cool Change*'s galley, circling in a practiced back-to-back waltz. She serves. He cleans up. They alternate telling funny stories, the other laughing, or hooting, or inserting a colorful detail. They sit against each other in the cockpit, hold hands in the moonlight.

The paradox of cruising is that as it expands your world, it also contracts it. The interior volume of your boat is almost certainly less than that of just the master bedroom in your home ashore. A talented designer can make the interior of a boat efficient and comfortable, even make it seem spacious, but there is no getting around the fact that you are going to spend a great deal of time in extraordinarily close proximity to those you cruise with. That can be good or bad, depending on the relationship.

The Relentless Sun

"He's thirty-four." Linda is telling you Paul's age.

"No!" You look toward *Sandpiper*. "I thought he was in his fifties."

"That's why," Linda says, tossing her head in the direction of the trimaran. Paul is on deck cleaning a conch, crouched over his own noon shadow. He wears only a Speedo. "He's been down here eight years and he's never had an awning on that boat. It has turned his skin to leather."

You look at Linda. Her skin seems creamy even in the shadow of the tent-shaped awning that spreads over *Figaro.* She reads your mind.

"I'm fifty-six. I just make it a point to keep something between my skin and the sun—an awning, sleeves, a wide-brimmed hat. And I use plenty of that." She points toward a large bottle of sunscreen sticking out of a canvas pocket in the cockpit. "Just common sense. You won't see any of the island women lying out in the sun in the middle of the day. Most of the older women still have great skin, and they've lived here their whole lives."

It is the sun that attracts vacationers to the tropics. Cruising to the tropics is another matter. Those with fair skin—really, anyone concerned with their skin (which should include all of us)—might regard the tropical sun as a major negative. Maybe, but later I'm going to talk a lot about the sun, including some life-extending benefits that may surprise you. I'm not soft-pedaling the consequences of too much sun—it is a killer—but avoiding excessive exposure isn't that difficult. Compare that with the break your lungs get from the air pollution you leave behind.

The point of all of this is that cruising, like almost everything else in life, has its good and its not-so-good. Every moment won't be—can't be—idyllic. But it is almost certain to be an improvement over what you leave behind, and it will be punctuated by periods of unimaginable contentment—a periodic taste of paradise.

Should you go? Only you can answer that. But if you do, even reluctantly, it is sure to be one of your most memorable experiences.

2

Confronting Fears

"WHAT IF SOMETHING HAPPENS TO KEN?" CAROL IS EXPLAINING TO ME HER anxiety about sailing.

"Like what?" I ask.

"Say, a heart attack."

"Do you think about that every time you get in the car with him?"

Carol's quick mind makes the logical leap, but her emotions resist: "It's different on the water," she insists.

"Right," I agree. "If Ken collapses on the boat, you've got an emergency all right, but he's the only one at risk. The same heart attack while he's driving is infinitely more dangerous—to both of you. And look, it's not just Ken. The driver coming the other way might be the one having the heart attack, but 100 or 1,000 times a day other cars flash by you a foot or two away and you hardly give it a thought. Just sitting on a street-side bus bench is more dangerous than sailing across the bay."

"Maybe it's the sense of helplessness," Carol ventures. "I'd probably just call 911; I always take the cellular."

"Exactly the same thing you'd do ashore," I point out.

"Yeah, but what about the boat?"

"It's not an airplane. You don't have to land it. Just drop the sails and you're parked. If you're in any danger of drifting ashore, start the engine or lower an anchor."

Carol absorbs this with a halfhearted nod.

Fear responds to reality like gray hair to Clairol—the effect is only temporary. You have to keep at it, or learn to live with the gray. But transient or otherwise, reality, like hair dye, is the only weapon we have. So let's talk.

Physical Danger

Water holds an undeniable attraction. Poets wax eloquent about the sounds it makes or the light it reflects. Couples find romance at its edge; the lonely find comfort. Homeowners pay premium prices for proximity. Travelers imagine the far shore.

But for most *Homo sapiens,* myself included, there is also something unsettling about it. Wide water is an alien environment. An open maw. A watery graveyard. It is home to giant waves, malignant currents, and violent weather, all waiting like a street gang for me to venture into the 'hood.

So how dangerous is sailing, really? Not very. Boating accidents, of which there are far too many in this country, almost invariably involve power-boats and alcohol or stupidity. Occasionally a sailboat is run down by one of these out-of-control admirals, but otherwise sailors rarely make the statistics.

But they do make the best-seller list. Every few years a liferaft story takes its place at the top of the current crop of "real life dramas"—those small-plane-crash, high-country-storm, car-in-ravine tales of survival. Such books are invariably a good read, but their cover pictures of storm-tossed seas or sunbaked rafters reinforce the fears of reluctant sailors.

The last unsinkable boat was the *Titanic.* Boats do sink, but most often they do it unattended. On those blue-moon occasions when a cruising boat does founder at sea, loss of life is rare, and appropriate preparation can diminish the risk.

Can I assure you that if you step aboard and head out across open water, you will undoubtedly arrive safe and unscathed at your destination? No one can give you that guarantee. But there is also no guarantee that today you won't slip in the shower or suffer a burst aneurysm in your brain. Life is full of danger. What I can tell you is that over the last 25 years Olga and I have met hundreds of cruisers, and not one of them has failed to reach shore safely.

Cruising is a relatively sedate activity. Don't confuse it with competitive sailing, where lightweight racing boats are driven through the worst weather and often pushed until they break—sometimes with disastrous consequences. While a good cruising boat can take far worse conditions than its light cousins, most cruisers prefer to ride gentle breezes from quiet anchorage to quiet anchorage. There is little about cruising that is inherently dangerous.

Perspective might be beneficial here.

- In the early-morning hours of August 24, 1992, an astonishing number of my "safe" shoreside friends crouched under shielding mattresses or huddled in interior bathrooms while Hurricane Andrew took a wrecking ball to their inland homes and shredded their neighborhoods into windrows of rubble. My friends survived, but the storm left 41 dead and 200,000 homeless.
- In 1993, friends in Iowa motored to safety in a bass boat as flood waters reached the eaves of their 60-year-old home. More than 23,500 *square miles* of "dry" land went underwater. Fifty people died and 74,000 lost their homes.
- In 1994, West Coast relatives were pitched from bed as shelves emptied themselves with a crash and walls let out the terrifying groan of bricks shifting against each other. Earthquake deaths worldwide average about 20,000 annually, which suggests that "solid ground" is an oxymoron.
- In 1995, Illinois experienced 76 tornadoes—53 in May alone. Nationwide the average is 700 tornadoes a year, causing 90 deaths.

The point of this litany? In more than 25 years of cruising, the absolute worst moments I've ever experienced were like a bad-hair day compared to any of these events. Bricks and mortar are not foolproof.

Perhaps you're willing to grant that *living* on a boat probably isn't inherently more dangerous than in a 3/2 ranch style in the suburbs, but once the docklines are aboard and the sails are up, we seem to be comparing apples to oranges. Am I really trying to make you believe that a small boat is a safe vehicle for traveling around the planet?

Actually, yes I am.

Where would *you* put a sailboat on the safety continuum? Safer than a hot-air balloon? Maybe safer than a motorcycle? How about safer than traveling by car?

Let's examine the facts. About 40,000 Americans die every year in traffic accidents, and nearly 6 million are injured. Fatal cruising accidents are almost nonexistent, and the rate of serious injuries is minuscule compared to 1 in 40 (6 million divided by 240 million). If you are inclined to throw up your own pristine driving record, let me point out that more than half of all traffic fatalities are innocent of any contribution; they are either passengers or the not-at-fault driver. Traffic statistics alone make a powerful case for giving up driving in favor of sailing.

There are no reliable statistics that will allow us to make a meaningful safety comparison between sailing and flying, but I will concede that the per-mile safety record of the airlines could be hard to beat. Still, 1996 was a particularly bad year for commercial aviation. More than 1,400 passengers died in seven separate airline crashes, and one-quarter of this horrific toll occurred in the United States. The significance is that even the safest means of travel is not without risk. Not to mention breathing for hours inside a closed compartment with 300 strangers.

Where does that place sailing? Much safer than driving, and if not demonstrably as safe as flying, at least healthier.

I could go on, citing office-building bombings and house fires, train accidents and carjackings, but you don't get over a fear of the dark unless you venture outside the circle of light. No matter how logically I make the case, fears about sailing probably won't go away until you're actually doing it. Just don't let them paralyze you.

You're Not Alone

Fear often has less to do with facing trouble and more to do with facing it alone. Carol finds reassurance in the cellular phone in her bag. If something bad happens, she can summon help at the touch of a button and turn the emergency over to someone trained to handle it.

Carol's strategy is fine for local sailing, but at sea the equation is different. You are likely to be on your own. Indeed, for those wanting to go, that is often one of cruising's appeals—a test of self with no one to bail you out if you get into trouble. It isn't that you can't summon help. The problem is that when an emergency occurs far offshore, the critical time may have already passed before help can arrive.

But . . . very little cruising time is spent at sea. On a typical cruise, you can expect to spend less than 2 percent of the time on passages that are longer than a day hop or the occasional overnighter. Equally to the point, more than 90 percent of your cruising time will be spent securely tied to something—an anchor or a dock—and while you can be alone if you want to, more often you'll be among other boats.

How many other boats? I'm glad you asked. About 20,000 "foreign" boats enter the waters of the Bahamas every year. That translates into a community of more than 40,000 (just in the Bahamas). Some events, such as the annual Family Island Regatta, can attract more than 500 boats to a single harbor.

The various islands of the eastern Caribbean also host several thousand cruising boats each winter. In addition, there is a huge charter fleet there, so being alone may be a problem all right, but not in the way you imagine.

Close to 1,000 sailboats transit the Panama Canal each year, about 60 percent west-bound. Some of those head north along the Central American coast to join several hundred West Coast sailors cruising the Sea of Cortez each year. Cabo San Lucas, at the southern tip of the Baja peninsula, has seen the number of visiting boats increase from just 35 in 1975 to more than 600 twenty years later.

Those with the time and inclination head west from Panama. Some stop at Darwin's Galápagos archipelago. The rest cross the Pacific to the fabled isles of Polynesia. About 400 sailboats per year enter Tahitian waters. Others choose Samoa, Fiji, or Tonga. Even if you decided to visit lonely Pitcairn Island, a once-mischarted speck of rock where the *Bounty* mutineers had hoped to avoid discovery, there is a good chance you won't be alone. It was once rarely visited but now three or four cruising boats a month call at Pitcairn during the safe season.

It isn't just the numbers. All cruisers are part of a community, in the most noble sense of that word.

Community doesn't mean much in America. Maybe you know your next-door neighbors (an astonishing number of us don't), but what about the people two doors away? Do you know anyone in the next block? If your car broke down a mile from your home, would you knock on the nearest door without hesitation? Would you feel safe to walk home?

In the cruising community everyone helps everyone. I don't know why that is. It's a chicken-or-egg issue: it could be that those drawn to cruising are generous by nature, or maybe cruising brings out the best in people. Or maybe it is the commonality. Whether we speak different languages, come from different generations, or have vastly different means, all cruisers have essentially the same concerns—weather, water, safe harbor, and supplies.

If you do go cruising, I'm not saying you'll like every other cruiser you meet. Life isn't like that. But no matter where you are, a rap on the hull of the nearest boat will get you help, not more trouble.

Blackbeard Drives a Lexus

The title was *Sitting Ducks*, and thankfully it had a shelf life only marginally longer than a quart of milk. In fairness, it wasn't a bad book—an account of the aftermath of a middle-of-the-night intrusion that left the author's cruising partner gravely wounded—but, oh, that title.

Are cruisers sitting ducks? I suppose, but here's the question. If you're a mallard anyway, are you safer preening on a Georgia farm pond a mile or so down the road from the Good Ol' Boys' Hunt 'n' Fish Club or on a lake in the northern Canadian wilderness, 100 miles from the nearest road?

America is the most violent peacetime country in the world. There is a violent crime in this country *every 17 seconds*. Assaults happen every 28 seconds, a robbery every 51 seconds. If you live in an American city and a drug addict breaks into your home and slashes you with a knife, don't expect to publish a book about it. Odds are the story won't even make the newspaper.

The sad truth is that Americans can go almost anywhere else in the world and be safer than they are in their own neighborhoods. The bar graph below dramatically illustrates this point.

Like here, the majority of crime in other countries occurs in their cities. If you spend most of your time anchored at the foot of villages and settlements—where everyone knows everyone—the likelihood of being the victim of anything more serious than petty theft is extremely remote.

Do you have kids? Did you know that gunfire is the second-leading cause of death among American children aged 10 to 19. *Gunfire!* And don't deceive yourself: less than half of these kids were minority. Of course the leading cause is auto accidents, so going cruising almost immunizes your children from their worst risks.

What about pirates? They aren't on the high seas much these days. They've found easier pickings selling cars, filing lawsuits, or sitting on city commissions. You might encounter a pirate when you're cruising—if you need a new battery or your refrigeration goes on the fritz—but he won't be armed with anything more lethal than the barrel he'll have you over.

The idea of evil lurking "out there" is Hollywood fiction. In cities you

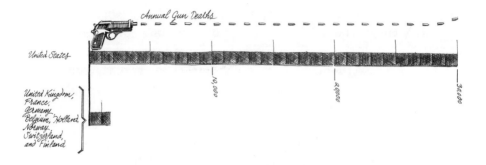

Annual Gun Deaths

United States

United Kingdom, France, Germany, Belgium, Holland, Norway, Switzerland, and Finland

10,000   20,000   30,000

run the same risk as any tourist, no matter how you arrive. In villages you are a guest and protected by the honor of all that live there. In remote anchorages you are alone. Period.

Assaulted by Nature

I was 26 the first time I spent a night offshore, and so nervous and frightened that I spent the early evening retching over the side of the boat. Exhausted and ready to move to Kansas, I lay down in the cockpit and tried to shut out the moment with my eyelids. Night fell, and when I opened my eyes, nothing in my 26 years had prepared me for the incredible beauty of the night sky viewed offshore away from any other source of light. The stars were so numerous that they were crowding each other for the tiniest bit of space. The Milky Way was a white road across the sky. The belt of Orion sparkled like a diamond bracelet. Without any frame of reference the stars seemed close enough to touch. I reached up like a child and tried to stir them with a circular sweep of my hand. Wonder displaced fear.

Eventually the sounds of the boat intruded on my skyward stare and I sat up. Ahead of us still more stars blinked off and on as the foot of the head-sail rhythmically rose and fell. Looking aft, I discovered that we were trailing fire as we sliced the warm, corrugated waters of the Gulf Stream. Luminescent plankton lit a billion torches as our boat shouldered them aside. Twin sparklers trailed 100 feet astern, the tiny torches apparently remaining alight until the dislocated plankton found their way safely home.

That was a long time ago, but I've never looked at the world quite the same since. I cannot tell you much else about that year, but the magic of that night is locked away forever.

What was I so afraid of on that first trip? It wasn't pirates. And it wasn't physical danger exactly, although drowning might have been on my mind. What I was really afraid of was the night. And the ocean. And the sky.

Life ashore is about image. If you don't really have the goods, you can fake it. Act like you know what's going on. Sound like you know what your talking about. Look cool. People are easy to fool. Look at how regularly community "leaders" turn out to be crooks, public "heroes" turn out to be scum.

Mother Nature is unimpressed with pretense. When she asks the questions, you damn well better know the right answers. That's what I was afraid of on that first night. Did I really know enough to be sailing across a pitch-black ocean? Would I prove capable or pay dearly for my impertinence?

I was conditioned to think of nature as a bully—spoiling plans, causing discomfort, even flying into a murderous rage. But ashore, at least, I had a masonry-underpinned, double-paned, climate-controlled refuge. Although I intended to keep my head down, what if she caught me out there, away from all protection? Would I know what to do? Would it be enough?

As night deepened, the wind strengthened, and our little boat buried her rail in the flaming foam. *Too much sail.* I *knew* what to do, but I was afraid to do it—and more frightened not to. With fatalistic determination I eventually fashioned a line into a harness, tied myself to the boat, and crawled forward to pull the genoa down.

It seems so elemental now, like adjusting blinds when the afternoon sun floods a room, but on that night the dramatic effect of reducing sail was a revelation. It signaled that the next two weeks would be less test and more seminar. Errors—and I made plenty—resulted in no more than anxiety, temporary discomfort, or cosmetic damage.

So was I assaulted by nature on that first trip? I have to say yes. There was the night sky and the phosphorescent wake. And in the morning the ocean changed to a blue clearer and more beautiful than the finest crystal. Pods of sleek dolphin surfed on our bow wave, arching clear in synchronized unison. When later we arched the other way, we discovered an undulating world of fascinating activity and dazzling color. Beaches we strolled were littered with shells as exquisite as inlaid jewelry. Silver showers would wash away all color, then the sun would gather it all and splash it across the immensity of the western sky. At night the ocean's shallow breath rocked us until the susurration of beach waves faded into profound silence.

I was incredibly egotistical to think of nature as a bully. Nature is, of course, completely indifferent to my existence. The only thing certain about the complicated equation that controls the ebb and flow of weather is that I'm not in it. Both metaphorically and in fact, how we get along in nature's fluctuating winds depends almost entirely on how we set our sails.

The Blush of Good Health

Away from familiar doctors and health facilities, illness can be a worry. It shouldn't be. Excellent health care is available in many parts of the world, and

rudimentary care is available in all but the most primitive locations. In the unlikely event of a serious illness, the American health-care system is rarely more than a few flying hours away.

Bowing to the wisdom of preparation, a later chapter details both prevention and treatment, but if you decide to cruise, you should anticipate health, not illness. For centuries doctors have prescribed ocean cruises to treat illnesses unresponsive to other therapies. Skeptics might conclude that this simply rids a doctor of troublesome patients, but I can attest that never have Olga and I gone cruising that we have not come back far healthier than we left. Cruising demands a good bit of physical activity, an essential element of good health.

Exercise, along with sunlight and fresh air, tends to whet appetites. Appetite might be a dirty word to you ashore, but when you satisfy it with a diet rich in seafood, one of the healthiest and least fattening, and when your day also includes vigorous physical activity, you have a recipe for replacing urban pallor with the glow of good health.

Because we are so acclimated to foul air, clean air typically is one of the least appreciated health benefits of cruising. The pristine air of most cruising grounds is a welcome and healthy purge for the pollution our lungs commonly deal with. This may not become apparent until the first time your cruise takes you to a city, where you will be appalled at the exhaust fumes. Remember that smell: you're going to smell it again when you get home.

Sea air is also pollen-free, making hay fever and most other allergies just a memory. And since you won't be in an office, elevator, or subway train every day, you won't contract every cold and flu that comes around. This is a particular blessing for small children.

Want to tighten your tummy or tone up your legs? It's easy: just jump over the side. Swimming and diving are an integral part of warm-water cruising, and no exercise gives a more complete workout than swimming. Swim every day and you will tone muscles you didn't even know you had.

Joggers will find beach running easier on the joints and harder on the calories. If it's upper-body development you're after, take over rowing duties in the dinghy. It's fun, it's healthful, it's peaceful, and it's free. Or put aboard a sailboard. It is easy to learn (really!), great fun, and an excellent upper-body workout.

Study after study links stress to an inordinate number of serious health problems, including stroke, heart attack, depression (suicide), and some cancers. Cruising stresses are short-lived—threading a channel, clawing down a sail, or maybe trouble with the engine. You deal with it and it's over. The rest of the time, if you're doing it right, cruising is relatively stress-free. No daily grind. No deadlines. No capricious boss to accommodate or unsympathetic goals to meet. *Floating convalescence.* If your shore life is stress-ridden, my guess is that every cruising day will add at least two days to your life span. Keep that in mind if you're a type A personality and think life is too short to "waste" a year of it on a cruise.

If you choose to cruise, the biggest risk to your health will likely be the sun. I'm not being facetious. The sun is a killer, and only farmers are more at risk. Yet if you learn to cover up, to protect your skin, and to take your sun in small doses, even it can be beneficial. For me, the choice between protecting myself from too much sun or trudging to the car in rain or sleet for that long, dangerous drive between work and home is no contest.

Close Quarters

Enforced proximity is sometimes a cause of concern. What's it like to spend 24-7 never more than a dozen yards from your cruising companion(s)? Won't the inevitable friction of such close contact result in chafe? And when tensions do build up, how do you "get away?"

On this subject nothing is quite the way it seems. For example, the only real confinement is when a boat is underway, but if a passage lasts long enough for forced proximity to be an issue, the reality is that a cruising couple will hardly have *any* contact—one sleeping while the other is on watch. Tensions are more common in port, where neighboring boats and shoreside diversions would seem to offer more than adequate opportunity for healthy separation. This empirically suggests that close quarters is not really the problem, but I would be disingenuous to leave it at that.

A couple ashore lead separate lives. They probably consult on "big things," but otherwise they are independent, going out into the world separately each morning. The cruising lifestyle provides a more intense relationship. Experiences are shared as they happen, not later over pot roast, and even the smallest choices require consensus—or dominance. Therein lies the rub.

When a couple trade life ashore for life afloat, the male half typically sees the transition as giving up one domain for another, or he may actually see cruising as giving up servitude for dominion. If we assume only one captain, that leaves the female partner trading sovereignty for serfdom. Such a deal. WAKE UP, GUYS.

Sharing intimately in the lives of those you love—spouse, children, or friend—can be cruising's best aspect. But it requires an understanding of the change in dynamics from life ashore. Failure to make the necessary accommodations bodes poorly for both the cruise and the relationship. We examine this issue in depth in the next chapter, but here's the relevant canon: if you are comfortable together ashore, expect the availability of time for each other and the mutual dependency that are part and parcel of cruising to nourish and invigorate your relationship. Conversely, if one of you is more at ease when the other partner is not around, a cruise is unlikely to help your relationship.

This doesn't mean you never want to be alone. We all benefit from some "alone time." You may be able to get it by losing yourself in a good book or clamping on a set of earphones. Otherwise, try solitary strolls on the beach, or if you prefer your time aboard, send the captain away for a few hours. No one should be offended by this.

There are fewer variables in the parent/child relationship, and the effect of a cruise is surer. Almost all parents report that cruising opens lines of communication between them and their children that are all but impossible ashore. Perhaps it is that the parents find they have more time for the children, time to understand the message instead of just the words. Perhaps it is the absence of external static on communication lines. Or maybe the opportunities for children to go wrong are fewer aboard. Whatever the reason, the vast majority of those cruising with children aboard share the opinion that cruising has been beneficial.

Discomfort

Cozy. That's the word those bitten by the cruising bug like. It's a spin word, an attempt to put the best face on a 7 × 7 living/dining room, a 3 × 3 kitchen. The interior of a well-designed cruising boat is indeed a study in efficiency, but there's no getting around the fact that it's, um, compact.

So if you have a nice house ashore, aren't you certain to be less comfortable moving into a space smaller than your bedroom? The short answer is yes, but it isn't the whole answer.

I like what Robin Lee Graham said at the end of his five-year cruise: "At sea I learned how little a person needs, not how much." Our shoreside pursuit of ever higher levels of comfort is a curse of modern life. Each year we Americans seem to work longer and harder, and for what? So we can be *more* comfortable? We want a larger house, a more luxurious car, the latest gadget that promises to make our lives easier, but when these things commit us to more hours on the treadmill, do they really make life easier?

The cruising life may be less comfortable, but it is more luxurious. When was the last time you slept until noon? When have you spent an entire day with a good book? Do you know what it's like to float for hours in warm, emerald waters? Do you know how wonderful bread is fresh from the oven? Is there a better combination than shade, breeze, food, and friends? How often do you toast the blush of sunset?

Luxury can be hard to appreciate when the cabin is so hot you can't breathe or your hair is as stiff as old Brillo, so a cruising boat must provide *sufficient* comfort. (I offer specific guidance in later pages.) Just keep in mind that a nest of pillows can be as comfortable as a leather recliner, 2 cubic feet of refrigeration is as good as 25 if it cools what needs cooling, and a shelf of books beats cable TV hands down.

Equal comfort? No. Discomfort? Sometimes. But rare is the cruising day that isn't, on balance, better than any day at the office.

Boredom

"What is there to do on a boat?" This may be the most asked question in a first encounter with the concept of cruising.

The answer is live. When the weather is good, the anchorage is abuzz with activities. Cruisers are socializing, heading off for sightseeing or shopping, sharing a sailboard, running the dog, or mounting a diving expedition. Depending on where you are, you can visit museums, try your luck at a casino, join a local festival, rent a motor scooter, sip wine on a shaded veranda, explore historic ruins, browse local markets, catch a matinee, bargain with street vendors, photograph wild flamingos, take a dayhike, or collect seashells.

Aboard the boat, in good weather or bad, you can read, listen to music, pursue a craft, practice an art, spend time on the radio, do required maintenance, bake, prepare elaborate meals, study a specific interest, keep a journal, write a book, play with your computer, learn a foreign language or a musical instrument—almost anything you might enjoy that you don't have time for now.

It is a new experience, having a whole day at your disposal day after day, but it doesn't take long to discover endless opportunities to fill those reclaimed hours with rewarding activity. Boredom? Not often, not if you have much zest for life. You are far more likely to find the days too short.

Dropping Out

Are you worried about losing ground (no pun intended) if you go cruising? Does it strike you as giving up your place in line for the next—what? Raise? Promotion? Opportunity? Employer contribution to your 401(k)? Are you afraid that friends will forget about you? Colleagues will sacrifice you? Those less deserving will pass you by? The kids will fall behind? The rosebushes will die?

Take a harder look. Will that raise do anything more than just let you "keep up?" Is the stress of additional responsibility what you really *want*? Aren't opportunities where you find them? Won't just eliminating dry cleaning save more than that piddling employer contribution?

Your *real* friends won't forget you. One of the first things the unbridled brain tosses is concerns about office politics. If you're off to the tropics, who is leaving whom behind? Do you think your kids will learn more about the world reading about it or actually seeing it? And as for those roses, what good are they if you don't take the time to smell them?

It is a shame that *dropping out* has such a negative connotation. A lifestyle you aren't happy with can seem as confining as prison. If that description fits you (or your partner), think of going cruising as *getting out*. If you are mostly happy with your life, you could think of cruising as *stepping out,* an invigorating change of pace. Sugar doesn't make the tea sweet; it's the stirring.

Perhaps the most accurate description is *finding out*. Those wanting to go believe cruising offers a chance to get more out of life. Those reluctant to go see it as putting "real" life on hold. Often it is not so much the truth about cruising that reveals itself in the relative silence and serenity of sail, but rather the truth about life.

Here is a truth Olga and I learned firsthand. For our first "test" cruise, we took a half-year sabbatical, returning to find that almost nothing had changed. Life ashore moves with the pace of a daytime soap. If you're gone a year, you can catch up in a week (if, when you get back, that's still what you want).

Whether it is aboard a sailboat or inside the stone walls of a Tibetan monastery, taking a little time out to consider life's bigger issues is worthwhile. Being away from everyday distractions allows a clarity of thought that often leads to pivotal inner discoveries. Don't worry about the world you leave behind; it will be essentially the same when you return. If anything of consequence changes, it will be you.

Failure

When I forsake terra firma, personal risk is never on my mind. I've checked the boat and know it's safe. I've checked the weather and feel confident that nothing dangerous is churning over the horizon. I know accidents can happen, but I feel 100 percent confident that I will survive. And if I don't, well, how is that any different from getting hit by a bus or discovering that I have inoperable cancer?

What nags at me is fear for the others aboard. The fact that Olga is clearly happy to be cruising with me doesn't override the knowledge that she wouldn't be out here except for me. Can a bad decision, a momentary lack of vigilance put her in jeopardy? This worry doesn't keep me from going, but it often makes me physically ill the first day of a cruise.

It was a long time before I discovered that fear of failure was just as strong for those dragged aboard.

Remember Carol? After our discussion about Ken having a heart attack, she brought up falling overboard.

"You mean Ken?" I asked her

"Yeah."

"Turn the boat around and pick him up."

"I'm not sure I could." *There it is.*

"Then the next time you go sailing, drop a cushion in the water and go back for it," I told her. "Keep doing that until you are sure."

"It's not the same thing. I might panic."

We humans are almost always better in an emergency than we expect, and Carol in particular is not the panic type. It wasn't panic she feared. She simply didn't think of handling a sailboat alone as something she could do, and she was rationalizing the spectacular failure she imagined.

Sailing a bus-size sailboat, particularly sailing it to distant ports, seems like it must be difficult, something that requires at least training, and maybe aptitude. For anyone pulled into such an enterprise, it must be akin to taking a new job in an unfamiliar field. The difference, of course, is that if you fail, you do it in front of the person you least want to disappoint.

What's to fail? Are you going to hit a dock? Everyone has done that. Accidental jibe? Nothing new there. Go aground? Not your fault unless you're the navigator. Seasick? You can join me at the rail. Petrified? It goes away. Panic in an emergency? It won't happen.

Give yourself a break. The challenges of cruising are no more difficult than those you deal with every day ashore. Cruising may change you, but it damn sure won't make you *less* competent.

Fear is a healthy emotion, but not if it keeps you from experiencing life. The cruising life is no more capricious than life ashore—and perhaps more worthy of risk. If fear is playing a part in your reluctance to at least give cruising a try, here is my best counsel: a good grip on a handrail and a good dose of common sense will ward off all but the most unavoidable misfortune.

3

Rights of Passage

A BOAT ON THE MOVE IS, IN MANY WAYS, A SOVEREIGN STATE, AND BEFORE YOU pledge your allegiance, you should have some idea of how it might be governed.

In 1776 Thomas Jefferson penned a single sentence destined to become the basis for a new nation:

> *We hold these truths to be sacred and undeniable; that all men are created equal and independent, that from that equal creation they derive rights inherent and inalienable, among which are the preservation of life, and liberty, and the pursuit of happiness.*

Despite Jefferson's noble creed, equality has been hard to come by for a lot of citizens. Women especially have made hard-won gains in achieving genuine equality.

If you are a woman, signing on to a cruise can seem like giving up those gains. It should not be so. You may indeed be dependent in the early days of a cruise—because of knowledge level, not gender—but if a cruise does not ultimately enhance your sense of self-determination, you aren't doing it right.

Oh Captain, My Captain

When a boat is underway, someone has to be in command. I'm not talking about who is steering. Someone aboard has to be responsible for getting the boat safely to the next destination. That person decides when to depart, what course to follow, what sails to set. He or she must keep track of where the boat is, pay attention and respond to changes in the weather, and recognize and avoid danger. He or she must look after the boat and make sure it is properly equipped and supplied. Confronted with an emergency, the captain must know how to respond and do it.

There is nothing radical about this concept. At the company where you work, someone is undoubtedly in command. It's how we coordinate efforts to accomplish a goal.

With only two (adults) aboard and only one *wanting* to be, it isn't hard to pick the captain out of this picture. Besides, it is part of his dream, captaining his own ship. And that's OK with you; you don't want to be in charge.

The problem is that unlike hired crew on a "real" ship, *you* are an equal partner. Being told what to do wears thin a lot quicker than you might think, and God forbid that the results of your efforts aren't up to the captain's expectations. It can be a big problem.

The overriding issue is safety—including yours. Handling a small boat on wide water sometimes requires decisive action. If a line (or a person) goes overboard at the bow, instantly disengaging the prop can avert disaster. Quick action in a sudden squall can avoid a frightening knockdown or costly sail damage. When the keel kisses the bottom, an immediate tack can, at the very least, save hours of sitting high and dry. In such circumstances there is no time for explanation or for democracy. Even when there is time for discussion, someone ultimately has to decide.

At sea the captain's word is law. That can be a hard pill to swallow when your captain is the same guy that doesn't notice the muffler has fallen off the car or can't find a shirt in his closet. It is especially hard to trust your captain when you know his experience is limited, but for a safe boat that's just what you have to do. Just keep in mind that your captain will be doing the best he knows how, and his primary concern will be with your well-being. If you doubt that, don't go sailing with this person.

The Bligh Syndrome

Some men turn into brutes when they step aboard a boat. They become overbearing, inflexible, and ill-tempered. They snap out orders like a prison guard and snap off heads when things don't go how they want. They wield their authority like a club, taking on the persona of a playground bully.

There are only two reasons for this behavior. Either this modern-day Captain Bligh is suffering from anxiety or he is a jerk. You know better than I.

If your partner is a jerk, put this book down now and forget about cruising—at least with him. Don't expect sailing to bring out latent good qualities; it won't happen. If he is a cad ashore, he will be infinitely worse in the confined spaces of a boat.

But even Mister Wonderful can turn into a petty despot on a boat, especially if he is a novice skipper. It is an all-to-common means of compensating for feelings of inadequacy. (The same kind of motivation makes some men abusers.) If he gets away with it, it can become his command "style." Don't let that happen.

If this problem crops up, deal with it early and decisively. Whether you need to soothe your frayed partner or jerk him up short depends upon your relationship. What you shouldn't do is put up with tyrannical behavior for very long.

Staying the Cat

At the slightest provocation, the real Captain Bligh was quick to subject members of his crew to the lash. Many of the seamen who eventually set him adrift in the ship's dinghy had the marks of the cat (cat-o'-nine-tails) on their backs.

While flogging has fallen from favor, you can still witness public lashing. I am embarrassed to admit how often I have seen some slob screaming at his crew about something they did or didn't do. More often than not the crewmember being tongue-lashed is a woman. It boils my blood.

Olga and I never shout and rarely even speak when we are handling our boat. For common maneuvers we have standard procedures, and for a new maneuver we discuss it well in advance. After that, all our communication is with half a dozen hand signals. It is a thing of beauty when we sail into a congested anchorage, plant the hook, and furl the sails in silence.

There are times when a shout would be in order. "DUCK!" comes to mind. And although my own tendency is toward disguising commands as requests—"Could you let that mainsheet out a bit?"—politeness can mask urgency. It would be a bit ludicrous to respond to seeing the bow light of a freighter looming overhead by saying, "Honey Bunny, I think we need to tack now. Would you spin the wheel over for me please?"

If you are on a boat very long, a time will certainly come when things go wrong. Maneuvering a sailboat is a bit like driving a car on ice, except that the skids and spins happen in slow motion. No matter how skillfully handled, a boat can suddenly head off in some unintended direction, usually right toward some solid object like a rock, a dock, or another boat. The shock of real-

izing that he is no longer in control can make the most taciturn captain suddenly strident. Experienced skippers bellow at the gods; the inexperienced bellow at the crew.

Yelling is almost always bad form, but you may need to cut a novice captain a little slack. Who hasn't reacted badly in a panic? If, however, this happens regularly, or even often, you need to call the captain's hand. It is true that, dragged aboard or not, to handle your boat smartly and minimize fiascoes, you need to be willing to take instructions. But no matter how quickly or slowly you "get it," there is never a reason to allow yourself to be subjected to the cat.

Exercising Your Franchise

Your participation in a cruise should be much more than just keeping the captain straight on appropriate protocol. Everything that happens on this cruise happens to you as well, so you are entitled to an equal vote. Don't hesitate to cast it.

You need to trust your captain on issues of safety, but enthusiasm, or sometimes obsession, can override common sense. A prime example is trying to beat bad weather to the next port. It is your life, too, so if the risk-to-reward ratio seems to you to be too high, it may be time to exercise your veto power.

Having said that, let me again point out that a well-found cruising sailboat is in little danger from the kind of weather a reasonable sailor might be tempted to risk. But bad weather is at least uncomfortable and can be downright terrifying. If you are aboard reluctantly, it can be in everyone's best interest to avoid "excitement" in those sensitive early days of a cruise. On the other hand, sailing in your first big wind will slay many lesser demons, so you might do yourself a favor to get it behind you at the first opportunity.

Ultimately, excitement is one of the attractions of cruising—a counterpoint to the typical tedium of life ashore—and many sailors come to treasure a "vigorous" sail. But it isn't fun until the boat feels safe to you. Once you're comfortable aboard, you will maximize your enjoyment by exploring your limits. You can go to a carnival without riding the rides, but it isn't much fun.

As with other activities, you get back from cruising what you put into it. If you take a passive role, you will miss some of the best parts of cruising. I'm not suggesting that you need to be "eaten up with it" like your gung ho partner, but researching the places on your route can add immeasurably to your visits there. Learning to sail the boat alone (it isn't that hard) can really boost self-esteem. Learning to dive opens up a world of unfathomable beauty. Learning to navigate connects you to the universe.

If you go cruising, go as an equal. And make the most of the experience.

By the way, if you become so inclined, there is no reason why you can't be captain. Successful cruising couples often achieve parity to the point that they become cocaptains—whoever is on watch is in charge. It is a nice arrangement, and represents a state of equality Jefferson could only write about.

Fulfilling Your Commitment

Captain or not, if you are aboard reluctantly, you are really the one in charge. The cruise succeeds or fails mostly on how you react to it. This puts both of you under pressure. Beyond the already considerable responsibility for your safety, the captain knows how tenuous your commitment is and worries that a single poor decision, or just bad luck, might appear to confirm your fears. For your part, you don't want your hesitancy to be a ball and chain on your partner's dream.

The wise captain will try to keep the early pace easy and concentrate on cruising's more conventional pleasures—sightseeing, sunning, and free time. Marina stops and even an occasional motel room might be a good idea. Most cruisers prefer the breezes and serenity of being at anchor to the heat and fishbowl atmosphere of a marina, but you are entitled to make the comparison for yourself. If someone aboard has done their destination homework, side trips away from the coast can make cruising seem less alien and more like ordinary travel.

Your responsibility is to make a genuine effort not to hold cruising to some unrealistic standard. Every day won't be a day in paradise. In fact, some days you may think you are at the other place. Just don't lose sight of the fact that bad days also occur ashore. When they do, maybe you make an adjustment, but you don't throw in the towel and make sweeping changes in your life. Sailing through a rough patch should likewise elicit a measured response.

Only a few cruisers carve out a permanent life afloat. For the vast majority a cruise is an episode in their lives, like going to college or living abroad. When they achieve their goals, or when they run out of time, money, or fun, they return to life ashore (although a significant number are soon planning their next cruise).

First-time cruisers often dream big. "We're going to buy a boat and sail around the world," they'll say. Some succeed; they're the ones you read about. But far more get only as far as the Bahamas or Baja, then return home embarrassed by their "failure." Failure? They lived aboard a boat and experienced life at its core for six months or a year while their colleagues trudged back and forth in the same old rut. How is that a failure?

It is the goal. If you tell family and friends you're going around the world and you don't, it feels like a failure, no matter how wonderful the cruise was. The solution is simple: no matter what dream burns inside, *stated* first-cruise plans should never be more specific than, "We've got a few months and we're headed south."

This, of course, is your partner's problem. Yours is just the opposite. If you don't make your commitment specific, it may be too easy for you to bail out at the first hint of discomfort. Cruises experience growing pains. You have to give a cruise time to mature. When that happens, you will both know whether you want to continue or stop. Until then, just take it a day at a time. There are sure to be some terrific days, and those that aren't won't seem nearly as bad when you look back at them.

Equal Employment Opportunities

One of the biggest gender problems aboard a boat can be the division of duties. A man steps aboard as captain. In addition, he handles most of the strength-demanding jobs like hoisting sails and anchors. He accepts responsibility for engine maintenance—mechanics being a traditionally male role—and he often reserves the role of navigator, perhaps, like captains of old, to protect his authority.

That leaves cooking, cleaning, laundry, and making beds for the mate. Oh boy.

Don't get me wrong. There can't be many jobs aboard a boat worse than bending yourself into a pretzel, inserting yourself into an airless, 110°F cockpit locker, and hugging a hot diesel engine, but a once-a-month oil change doesn't offset preparing three meals a day. Not by a long shot.

An equitable labor division should be part of the early planning. Reel in your ego; one job is just as important as another. The issue here is fun; don't get stuck with more than your fair share of the unpleasant jobs aboard.

Fortunately few tasks are universally repugnant. Maybe you can't see the appeal of a trip to the top of the mast, but you find varnishing both therapeutic and rewarding. If your partner loves to go up the mast and hates to varnish, these two are easy to assign. If this cruise is your partner's dream, barring physical barriers he is likely to take on all handling and maintenance duties without complaint, accepting whatever assistance you want to offer. The bigger problem—for you—is domestic duties.

If you like to cook, cruising provides the time to indulge your passion, and everyone aboard will love you for it. If your partner is the cook, then except for when the boat is underway, the galley should be his responsibility. If you both hate to cook, you'll need to strike a compromise: you can't get a night off by ordering Chinese.

A common onboard rule is that the cook doesn't do dishes. This can have the unplanned effect of awakening a latent interest in cooking.

Other domestic duties, such as cleaning and laundry, are less relentless than cooking and dishwashing, but if you don't enjoy them, try to trade them off for something you like better. For example, I don't mind doing laundry in a bucket, so that is one compensation I make for having no culinary talent whatsoever (unless it involves charcoal). As for cleaning, Olga and I do that together—both inside and out.

Allow me a small digression. "I can't cook" shouldn't get your partner out of KP duty anymore than "I can't sail" would disqualify you from cruising. Anyone that can read can follow a recipe and turn out edible fare. A cook, however, can add the right spice, make the right substitution, or put together the right combination to make a meal special. Someone with "the touch" may find cooking aboard more rewarding than expected because of the importance meals take on in the elemental atmosphere of cruising. The melancholy of a rainy day, for example, can be swept away with a fine meal. If meal preparation becomes an art form for either of you, cultivate it. You will have a happier ship for it.

Female domesticity is not always the man's fault. Women unsure of themselves on a boat sometimes retreat into the domestic duties, and the captain, not wanting to look a gift horse in the mouth, lets it happen. Bad gambit. Eventually you are almost certain to resent being shackled to the galley, but by then this arrangement will be well entrenched. Even worse, you compro-

mise your own safety if you don't have at least a cursory knowledge of how to operate the boat. Don't put yourself in this position.

Because cruising is about doing most things together, couples (and families) tend to achieve an equitable balance soon enough, but having a degree of sensitivity to this issue from the start can avoid early resentments. Equality is easier to achieve on a boat than ashore. Ironically, so is inequality. Which you realize depends mostly on you.

Bill of Rights

What are your inalienable rights? Jefferson lists ". . . the preservation of life, and liberty, and the pursuit of happiness." Those are the big ones all right, but let's get more specific.

You have the right to sail on a safe boat. That means sensible design and quality construction. You can sail coastal waters in almost any cockleshell, but if your cruise will take you offshore, your boat should be strong and seaworthy. Unless you want to familiarize yourself with the tenets of design and construction, you have to take your partner's word about your boat's suitability, but if you have doubts, get a second opinion.

Even if your boat is strong enough to crush rocks, it isn't safe unless it takes care of you. Make sure the decks provide secure footing. Smooth fiberglass anywhere you are likely to step is treacherous. Molded nonskid loses traction with wear. Teak decks look nice oiled but can be slick. Wet the deck and try to slide. You should stick like a tree frog; anything less isn't safe.

Every cruising boat needs sturdy double lifelines encircling the deck. Some suggest their omission makes you pay more attention to holding on, and thus you are actually safer without them, but by that argument you would be safer in a high-rise apartment if you removed the balcony railing. Poppy-cock. Make sure your boat's lifelines are tall, tight, and in good condition.

One other essential feature of a safe boat is an adequate number of strong handholds. You should be able to go from stern to bow without releasing your grip. Below, you should be able to traverse the cabin like a kid on the ladder rungs of a jungle gym. Too many factory-installed handrails are a stretch even for a 6-footer. If handhold spacing is too wide, above or below, tell your skipper it is time to get a grip.

You have the right to essential equipment in working order. The boat must obviously satisfy Coast Guard requirements for navigation lights, flares, fire extinguishers, life jackets, and the rest, but additional items should be aboard for your safety. Adequate charts and navigational gear are essential. There should be a safety harness aboard that fits you. Likewise, life jackets should fit. You should have effective man-overboard gear. A safe bosun's chair is essential for trips up the mast. There must be ample strong ground tackle aboard for secure anchoring, and a windlass may be needed for you to get it back aboard. Sheet and halyard winches should be powerful enough for you to hoist and trim the biggest sail.

Cruising is about self-sufficiency, and most cruisers believe that if you get yourself into a tight spot, you should make every effort to extract yourself before looking for someone to rescue you. I tend to agree, but I also realize that if you are dragged aboard, such logic doesn't apply. So be sure your boat has a VHF radio aboard. And if your cruise will take you out of VHF range— more than 50 miles from shore—you should also be equipped with an EPIRB (emergency position-indicating radiobeacon).

What about a life raft? That's a harder call. We look at life rafts and alternatives in a later chapter, but if after you consider all sides of this question you don't feel safe without one, then it should be aboard.

A cruise is often a tight-budget endeavor, and that can lead to inadequate maintenance. It is fine to cruise on a budget—the essentials of cruising aren't expensive—but everything aboard that you will depend on must be in top condition. For example, an engine isn't necessarily essential—you can cruise without one—but if you expect to depend on it, then it must be maintained without compromise. If you can't keep your boat in top shape on the available funds, you need a smaller or a less complicated boat.

You have the right to expect your captain to be competent and knowledgeable. If your partner is a longtime sailor with thousands of sea miles in

his wake, this is an easy one. But if most of his sailing has been on the Sea of Imagination and the only thing salty about him is his vocabulary, he owes you certain assurances.

Seamanship is an acquired skill; you can't become a good seaman without going to sea. But innumerable volumes have been written that can help the novice avoid the most egregious mistakes. If your captain is a novice, his nightstand ought to be stacked with boating books.

What should the captain know? He should know the Rules of the Road. He should be able to read a chart. He should understand tides and currents, and have some understanding of weather patterns. He should possess basic piloting skills and be able to plot a course.

If your cruise will take you offshore, the captain must be able to determine the boat's position—by more than one means. He should have enough familiarity with all the boat's essential systems to diagnose problems and make repairs. He should be competent to deal with an emergency.

The captain should know how to sail and how to anchor. Seamanship skills must include knowing what to do in deteriorating weather, when and how to reduce sail, and how to navigate in fog, rain, and darkness. And he should know exactly what to do if someone goes overboard (and so should you).

The novice skipper doesn't come aboard with all of these skills, but if he has learned enough to have the confidence to sail a boat boldly and he has the patience to sail it wisely, he is unlikely to get you into serious trouble.

You have the right to sail only on tranquil seas. If someone drags you aboard on their cruise, they have almost certainly promised you that it will be fun. By definition that excludes risking a North Atlantic gale or a tropical cyclone (hurricane or typhoon). You won't be able to avoid local disturbances, but global weather patterns are reasonably predictable. Your cruise should take you into areas subject to gales and cyclones only during their safe seasons.

Your cruise should also avoid political storms. A few parts of the world can be unsafe in any season. None of these "hot spots" should be on your list of ports of call.

You have the right to be dry, rested, and well fed. These are the essential elements of being comfortable underway. They suggest that your boat will not leak and should have some means of protecting the on-watch crew from flying spray. It should have dry, secure, comfortable bunks well aft (to minimize motion) that allow the off watch to rest. And the galley should be capable of turning out nourishing meals in all but the worst conditions.

These are universal rights. You may want to include others in your constitution. If you want a discretionary fund or the right to fly home periodically, you will never be in a stronger negotiating position than now. Try your amendment and see if you can get it to pass.

4

Home Sweet Home

FROM HERE WE PROCEED AS THOUGH A CRUISE IS IN YOUR FUTURE. THE remainder of this book is about how to make cruising work best *for you*. Whether you are going aboard with tentative enthusiasm or entrenched reticence, much that follows is sure to improve your lot.

This chapter is about accommodations. I know I promised no technical boat discussions, but even a conventional tourist expects hotel rooms to meet certain requirements. You should expect no less from the cabin of a cruising boat. To the extent that we are talking about the boat's function as a home, helping you make it as comfortable as possible seems appropriate.

Open Interior

Old-house renovation almost always starts with taking out a few walls to "open" the floor plan and make the interior feel more spacious. If ever there was a living space that benefits from this logic, it is the interior of a boat. Efforts to make the cabin seem spacious are hard enough; dividing 300 square feet into three or four rooms is not helpful.

If you already own the boat you plan to cruise, there may be little you can do about the interior layout. If you are going to buy a boat, you have a few more options, but all boats make compromises. The guiding tenet is that the cabin will be plenty "cozy" without dividing it into smaller spaces. Look for an open layout.

This doesn't mean eliminate the head enclosure; some privacy is essential. But the longer your views, the less confining the cabin will feel. Although you may be attracted to their privacy, "staterooms" in a 30-something or even a 40-something boat shrink the size of the salon—your main living space. Even the privacy attraction soon fades when you take the boat into a warm climate. For life below the deck to be tolerable in the tropics, efficient cross-ventilation is essential—difficult to achieve in a small stateroom with the door closed.

Open cabin doors are the norm, but they often block access to a locker or cabinet located behind them. If this is the situation aboard your boat, consider removing the door(s) and leaving it (them) ashore. A removable curtain can serve occasional privacy needs just as effectively without the daily inconvenience of the door.

What about guests? Aside from the fact that aboard a small boat privacy is mostly illusory whereas the effect of blocked ventilation is not, it is almost always a bad idea to make guest accommodations a major concern. Configure the cabin to give yourself daily use of all available space. A convertible area will be adequate for occasional guests—not unlike the pull-out sofa ashore. If that offends your sense of hospitality, give your guests the "good" bunk. Just don't commit precious real estate to them when they aren't there.

Layout requirements are somewhat different for the cruising family. Children need their own space, and so will you for that matter. With more than two people aboard, some cabin separation becomes more desirable.

Ventilation

I love those pictures of a crimson hull against the blue-white of ice cliffs, and I admire sailors who take their boats above the arctic circle, but I don't envy them. Like most cruisers, I am attracted to warmer parts of the globe—hot even—and that necessitates good ventilation in the boat that takes me there.

No matter where your cruise is headed, it is worth considering that you can always close opening portlights, but you can't open fixed ones. Likewise, deck hatches are almost as valuable for the light they admit on a dreary winter day as for their hot-weather ability to funnel cooling breezes below deck.

All boats need passive ventilation. When you're aboard, you need fresh air to breathe. Equally important, the boat needs to breathe even when you aren't aboard. As sunlight heats the deck and hull, the warming cabin air sucks in moisture from the outside. The air inside a closed boat on a hot day can be *three times* as wet as that outside. This moisture isn't expelled when the air temperature cools at night. Instead it condenses out—like dew—wetting everything in the cabin. A few days of this and bunks are damp, clothes are clammy, and mildew is rampant. It also damages the boat. Tell the captain that Meade Gougeon reportedly rates excess moisture trapped below decks as the single worst problem with the overwhelming majority of today's boats.

Be sure the cabin has at least two ventilators (so dry air can flow in as the wet flows out) that can stay open in all weather. Cowl vents on Dorade boxes meet this requirement.

Boats at anchor normally *weathercock*—point into the wind—but they can't do this tied up in a slip. The effect of water currents on the hull can also cause the boat to lie crosswise to the wind. In either case, a boat with fixed ports will be stifling below deck, while opening ports will let the cross-breeze blow right through the cabin. Imagine a house in Florida with no air conditioning and windows that don't open. For comfort, at least some of the ports should open; for safety, they should be strong.

The big gun in boat ventilation is the deck hatch. Opened into the stream of air, a deck hatch pours cooling breezes into the cabin. Fitted with a fabric "scoop," a deck hatch can catch the slightest zephyr and send it below.

Unless the cabin is totally open, a single hatch (plus the companionway) will prove inadequate in the tropics. Don't expect any hatch not in your line of sight to send much air your way. The breeze is always the strongest as it comes through the hatch, so ideally wherever you are in the cabin, you want a hatch right above you. One above your bunk is essential. One above the galley will vastly improve the chef's disposition. One above the main settee will add im-

measurably to the pleasures of dining, entertaining, reading, or vegetating. The benefits of a hatch in a booth-size head need no amplification.

Unless you plan to run a generator around the clock, deck hatches are the closest you will get to air-conditioning. Be sure your boat has an adequate complement of hatches. If it doesn't, additional hatches are simple enough to install.

Comfortable Seating

If I were building a boat from scratch, I would eliminate one settee and replace it with a pair of comfortable swivel chairs—recliners if the boat were large enough. It is shocking how little *comfortable* seating—if any—most production boats have below deck.

You are going to spend a lot of time sitting below, so give this some attention. Buy yourself a thick new paperback and spend an entire Saturday sitting in the cabin reading. If your hipbones are soon grinding into the plywood beneath the cushion, or your back is in spasms, changes are needed.

Loose cushions may have the wrong type of foam. Factory cushions can be too thin or too soft (soft foam is cheaper). Cushions on a solid base should be at least 4 inches thick, and you need firm polyurethane (open-cell) foam. Foam goes soft with age, so if you buy new foam, firmer is better. If the foam is designated by weight, try 50- or 60-pound as a starting point. Backrests can be softer if they don't double as sleeping cushions.

Some boatowners select closed-cell foam because it won't absorb moisture, but closed-cell foam deflates as you sit on it, becoming harder as you sink into it. Closed-cell foam is the only choice for cockpit cushions, but it is significantly less comfortable than polyurethane foam for sitting or sleeping.

The angle of the backrest is critical. Making back cushions wedge-shaped works fine unless the back cushion doubles as a bunk cushion. In this case, a wedge-shaped filler behind the back cushion can give it the proper angle.

The easiest and often the most effective way to make cabin seating comfortable is with pillows. Bed pillows, toss pillows, even special lumbar rolls can allow you to build a comfortable nest in the corner of an otherwise inhospitable settee. Take a few pillows with your novel and see if you can find a truly comfortable combination, then be sure those pillows get aboard.

Good Lighting

My first cruising boat had kerosene cabin lights. So romantic!

Yeah, right. And so hot. And such a case of eyestrain.

Leave romantic lighting to restaurateurs. You want electric light, and plenty of it.

The captain will prefer fluorescent lights because they give the most illumination for the electricity they consume. Some people find their light harsh, but because fluorescents are also cool you may be inclined to overlook this aesthetic in the heat of the tropics. The light from incandescents is warmer, but they give off a lot of heat. Halogen lights are brighter, but also hotter.

Good cabin lighting is like good home lighting: you need both "room" lighting and task lights. Fluorescent fixtures mounted on the overhead provide the most efficient area lighting. Fluorescents also work well as counter lights in the galley. Small incandescent or halogen fixtures can provide focused light for navigation and reading.

Deck hatches provide the best daytime lighting. For a dark area without a hatch, consider installing a deck prism. A thin piece of clear acrylic (Plexiglas) custom-cut to replace the companionway dropboards will immeasurably improve the cabin light—and cheer—on rainy days.

As the boat swings on her anchor in the daytime, patches of direct sunlight will sweep the cabin like prison searchlights until they find your face. It is one of those Murphy's Law things. Portlights will need curtains, blinds, or snap-in-place block-out panels. Canvas "eyebrows" are another option, also allowing ports to remain open when it is raining. Deck hatches are often shaded by an awning, but otherwise canvas covers are effective.

Pleasant Decor

I don't presume a special knowledge of interior decoration, but a few rules do apply.

First, light colors expand a space, dark colors contract it. Go aboard a boat with dark wood bulkheads and dark upholstery and it feels like a cave,

no matter how beautiful the wood. Give the same cabin white bulkheads with light-wood trim and bright upholstery fabrics, and it will seem open and cheerful. Boat cabins are too small for their primary colors to be dark.

If the interior of your boat features a lot of dark wood, counter it with light-colored fabrics. With white or light-colored bulkheads you have a broader range of upholstery-fabric choices. Dark cushions tend to show the abuse of daily use less. Random patterns hide stains, but a "busy" pattern in motion can make you queasy.

Experts recommend a color scheme with an odd number of colors for the most pleasing effect. If you are headed for the tropics, use cool colors (green, blue, violet) in the cabin. Everything is so bright, vivid, and hot down there that cool colors in the cabin will be a welcome respite. Trust me.

Fabrics

It wasn't that long ago that boats were all delivered with vinyl-covered cushions. The idea was that the vinyl wouldn't absorb moisture, and the cover could be wiped dry. Oh man, anyone who has ever owned a piece of vinyl-covered furniture knows it is both cold and hot, and it sticks to bare skin like surgical tape. Sleeping on a vinyl mattress—even one covered with bed linens—is pure torture.

Cotton is wonderful, but it readily picks up moisture, and it is prone to mildew. It is also subject to shrinkage. Cotton fabrics that are preshrunk and treated to resist mildew aren't bad boat fabrics.

The best boat fabrics are synthetics, or a mix of synthetic and natural fiber. Some of these fabrics are pleasant to the touch, stain resistant, and wear like iron. Being washable is a plus. Any fabric you would use on a sofa that gets daily hard use in your home should work equally well on the boat.

If reupholstering is part of your precruise program, buy a couple of yards of your chosen material and sit on it, sleep on it, and spill on it. Fold it in half and cut two squares simultaneously, then wash one of them. Compare it to the unwashed one for shrinkage and color change. If the fabric passes these tests and you still like it after looking at it every day for a couple of weeks, you'll have much more confidence in your selection.

Galley

I don't mean to make any presumption here: if the galley won't be your responsibility, you can leave it to whoever will be feeding the ship. However, if by choice or default you expect to be in charge of culinary activities, give the galley as much scrutiny as you would the kitchen in a new home, because that is precisely what it is.

Oddly enough, a compact galley is preferable to an expansive one. Boats move around, and losing your balance is especially hazardous in the presence of hot pots. It is essential to be able to wedge yourself securely when cooking so that an unexpected lurch doesn't send you flying.

Good galley design minimizes floor space to confine your movement while maximizing counter space to provide plenty of work area. This is achieved most efficiently with a U-shaped galley, which surrounds the cook with workspace. In the best design the U is open either forward or aft, allowing the cook to brace against a counter on either tack. Space limitations make an opening to the side more common, but this configuration can be equally efficient except on one tack.

L-shaped galleys put a third less counter space in immediate reach. In a narrow boat a Pullman galley—counters on either side—can be as efficient as an L-shape and better underway. A side galley—meaning a single straight counter along one side of the hull—requires the most movement from the cook, but the short distances in all galleys make this a fine distinction. Olga and I have cruised with a side galley for 20 years.

Outfitting the galley is a different chapter, but counter space on your boat won't be lost to appliances. Minimally you need enough counter space to prepare food, to drain dishes, and to set hot pans off the stove. Hinged or slide-out sideboards can give added counter space when needed.

Counter surface. Plastic laminate, the most common counter surface, gives excellent service. Stainless steel also makes a good counter, particularly when the sink is integral so that it provides a true "drain board." Varnished wood looks pretty, but it is a poor choice for a galley counter. Tile makes a nice work surface if the counter isn't too large; weight added as a countertop is that much less in supplies the boat will carry. For the same reason, stone (marble or granite) isn't practical until the boat is quite large. Use solid surface materials like Corian or Fountainhead to get the look of stone without the weight.

Straps and bars. There should always be a safety bar between you and the stove. For cooking underway, anything but a fore-and-aft U-shaped galley should also be equipped with a sturdy safety belt to hold you in place. The usual configuration is a foot-wide belt clipped to sturdy eyebolts at each end of the counter, but clipping a harness to a bar across the face of the counter lets you more easily sidestep hot spills.

Sinks. A lively boat will toss the water right out of a shallow sink. The galley sink should be deep, and large enough to hold the biggest pot aboard. The main benefit of a double sink is that it provides a secure place to drain dishes, but extra counter space may be more valuable in a small boat.

Sinks need to be located near the centerline of the boat. Otherwise,

when the boat heels deeply the sink dips below the waterline (which points out the worst feature of a side galley). Closing the seacock prevents the boat from flooding, but then you no longer have a sink that drains. Sitting the boat upright every time you need to drain the sink is a pain.

Garbage. Garbage is another pain. Small bits of organic matter—food scraps—can be fed to the fish, and tin cans make good marine habitats (in deep water only, please!), but everything else needs to go into an odor-tight container to be bagged and disposed of ashore, meaning deposited in a garbage receptacle, not buried on the beach. As you cruise, you will learn to minimize the amount of garbage you generate—one of cruising's many conservation lessons—but you still have to deal with the garbage you do have.

Garbage cans that drop into a countertop fitted with a lift-off lid are convenient but take up cabinet space and need to be sealed effectively from the cabinet interior. Tilt-out garbage containers provide similar convenience with the same sealing requirements. Hanging-bag systems on a cabinet door can work if you don't overload them. Sometimes the engine hatch has dead space that can be adapted into a garbage receptacle, but be sure you don't create a fire hazard. The easiest alternative might be a lidded kitchen trash can placed out of the way, like under the companionway ladder. Just be sure your galley includes a place for garbage.

Water

The measure of wealth on a cruising boat is in gallons, not dollars. The more fresh water you have available, the more luxurious your life afloat will feel. This is especially true in the dry, "blue sky" parts of the world favored for cruising.

Why not carry all the water you can use, even if you have to fill up every couple of weeks? Because enough water to accommodate the average *onshore* consumption of two people for two weeks would fill the interior space of a

35-foot boat *more than 3 feet deep*—not to mention that the water would weigh more than the boat.

Adding some capacity may be possible, but the installation of an additional water tank brings an equal reduction in storage space for other essentials. Compact watermakers that convert seawater to fresh water are available, but they are expensive to buy, consume a lot of electricity, and are not immune to problems. Often the most practical approach is to concoct strategies to comfortably reduce your consumption to a level consistent with the water capacity of your boat.

Salt water. The water you *use* in two weeks ashore would fill a 10-foot-diameter backyard swimming pool, but what you *ingest* in that time wouldn't overflow a good-size kitchen sink. Recognizing the magnitude of this disparity will help you adapt to limitations cruising imposes.

Substituting seawater has the most dramatic effect on onboard consumption, often without consequence. For example, toilets flush equally well with seawater. If the water you are afloat in is clean, it will wash dishes as well as that in your tanks. It is better than fresh water for brushing your teeth. Some seafood is better cooked in seawater.

Every sink aboard should have a saltwater spigot.

Foot pumps. "Running" water is convenient but wasteful. Consider how much water goes down the drain while you brush your teeth. It is possible to be conservative with pressure water, but it isn't easy; running-water systems are designed to run. Something as simple as washing hands requires you to turn the water on to wet your hands, then back off while you lather. Now you have to turn the tap with a soapy, dirty hand to restart the flow for rinsing your hands, including throwing some water up on the handle to clean it. If you must have pressure water, at least install single-lever faucets.

Hand pumps may make you more conservative because you have to pump every drop, but they are infuriating to use. Washing one hand while you pump with the other one is like clapping with one hand—it just doesn't work. Nor does washing dishes one-handed. Don't cruise with hand pumps.

A foot pump lets you have your hands under the faucet before the water flows, lets you control the flow precisely, and lets you rinse without soiling anything but the bottom of the sink. It frees both hands to deal with a heavy pot, to support a colander, or to cup a mouthful of water for rinsing your teeth. A well-placed foot pump is more convenient than pressure water, and it will halve the water usage of even the most conservation-minded crew. The ideal water-delivery system for a cruising boat is twin spigots supplied by side-by-side salt-water and freshwater foot pumps. This arrangement supplies you with unlimited seawater, and it gives you precise control of your freshwater usage.

Foot pumps are less convenient to supply water to a shower head. A small on-demand electric pump can supply adequate pressure for a satisfactory shower without stressing water (or battery) capacity. A handheld shower head lets you concentrate the water where you want it. For an even stingier shower, consider putting a pressurized lawn sprayer aboard; it will provide an amazingly satisfying freshwater rinse on a pint or two of water.

Hot water. The typical boat water heater uses heat from the engine to warm the water in the tank. A second heating element—an electric one—works only when the boat is plugged in at a dock or running a big generator. If you run the engine every day to charge batteries or chill the refrigerator (a common requirement), you can also make hot water, and a well-insulated water heater will maintain its heat for much of the day.

Water heaters, however, have a couple of significant disadvantages. First, they require a pressure water system to keep the tank full; otherwise the heating element will burn out. Second, the water in the line to the faucet soon cools, so a lot of water can be wasted while waiting for the water to run hot. Both of these problems can be overcome (pressurize just the hot water and mount the heater closer to the faucets), but they rarely are.

Because the need for on-demand hot water is modest—water limitations are likely to prohibit using hot fresh water for dishes, laundry, or long, hot showers—it can be more sensible to meet your hot-water requirements with a kettle. When Olga or I set the morning coffee off the burner, we quickly bring a kettle to boil, then pour the steaming water into a pump thermos mounted in the galley. It provides us with ample hot water all day, with no water wasted and no need to run the engine. For a warm shower—hot showers are not highly regarded in the tropics—we add a small amount of boiling water into our shower/sprayer.

Another option in the tropics is a deck-mounted day tank painted black and plumbed into the galley. A flat 15-inch by 15-inch tank 2 inches high will hold about 2 gallons. The sun-heated water will flow into the galley by gravity. The only energy requirement is refilling the tank every couple of days.

On-demand gas water heaters are also available but so dangerous on a boat that they should not be considered.

Rain catchment. Rain catchment is not technically an interior design issue, but good rain-catching strategies can make life aboard much more like life ashore. Full water tanks will contribute as much as any design feature to your sense of contentment and well-being. At the very least, your harbor awning should be fitted with a drain at its lowest point(s) that can be connected to a hose to route rain to your tanks. Many cruisers build special catchment awnings that are less subject to tossing the water out when wind accompanies the rain.

A passive way of collecting rain that is completely unaffected by wind is to dam the deck scuppers and route all the water that lands on the deck into the tanks. This strategy does require keeping the deck scrupulously clean and allowing the first of the rain to wash salt off the deck before you send the water into the tanks. Damming just the cabintop reduces the deck-cleaning burden.

You take fresh water for granted until you live where the supply is no longer unlimited. Make sure you will have at least "enough"—however you may define that.

Stoves

Diesel, coal, and even wood-burning galley stoves can be wonderful shipmates in a cold climate—so they tell me. But when the outside temperature climbs above 50°F, you no longer need to put the bread in the oven to bake it; just leave it on the counter. If you have an "ice" cruise in mind, you should research solid-fuel stoves and their diesel stepsisters. But if your cruising itinerary is more conventional, you have only two choices—kerosene or propane.

What about alcohol? I suppose manufacturers install alcohol stoves because they are "safe," meaning they are unlikely to explode. They do catch fire with alarming frequency, but it is easy for liability attorneys to convince jurors whose fault *that* must have been. In fairness, alcohol stoves are relatively safe, and alcohol fires can be extinguished with a douse of water.

While alcohol stoves may be fine for warming soup, brewing coffee, and even cooking a meal or two on a weekend aboard, they are a terrible choice as a galley stove on a cruising boat. Alcohol burns far too cool for cooking, taking the adage "a watched pot never boils" to an entirely new level. They are inconvenient to use, needing to be pressurized with a hand pump and requiring the burner to be preheated—by burning raw alcohol in a "priming" cup—before the burner can be ignited. Burning alcohol gives off an odor that makes many seasick. Burners are subject to failure, quickly choking on any impurities in the fuel. Suitable alcohol is expensive and unavailable in many places. In the Caribbean you may be driven to burning high-proof rum in your stove, which clogs burners and is a shameful waste of rum. If your boat is equipped with an alcohol stove, convert it to kerosene or replace it with a gas stove before you leave.

A kerosene stove, sometimes called a Primus stove, operates much the same as an alcohol stove, needing to be pressurized and primed before the burner can be lighted. And priming is usually done with alcohol, so even the sickening smell of burning alcohol is not completely eliminated. But kerosene has two enormous advantages over alcohol.

First, pressurized kerosene burns roughly twice as hot as pressurized alcohol, cutting cooking times in half. Second, kerosene is available all over the world—although the quality in some third-world countries is so poor that burning it soon clogs the burners. But a gallon of fuel will run the stove for about 30 hours, so it isn't hard to carry a four-to-six-month supply of fuel aboard, replenishing whenever clear kerosene is encountered.

Liquefied petroleum gas (LPG)—usually propane—is the most convenient cooking fuel by far. Like kerosene, LPG is available almost everywhere, although differences in fittings can make getting it from the supplier's tank into your bottle problematic. It is easy to use—just turn the knob and light the burner. The heat is adjusted by lowering the flame (lowering the heat on a kerosene stove requires the insertion of a "flame tamer" under the pot). Ovens have a "ring" burner, and can even be equipped with a broiler. And a gas stove, as every chef knows, is a joy to cook on.

LPG is also—by far—the most dangerous cooking fuel. Propane and butane are heavier than air, so they "spill" like water. Leaking propane in a house falls to the floor, usually dispersing harmlessly on air currents, but a boat is like a bowl, and leaking gas accumulates in the bottom of it. One spark and KA-BOOM!—shattered fiberglass rains down like a ticker-tape parade.

I think the risk is too high and live with kerosene—the operative word here being "live." But I am in the minority: most cruisers choose LPG, and almost all of them survive that choice. A safe installation and good habits minimize the risks.

Here are the rules. Propane bottles should be on deck, but if the captain insists on putting them in a locker, the locker must be isolated from the rest of the boat and have a drain (that doesn't go underwater when the boat heels) to let leaking gas escape over the side. The first thing connected to the valve on top of the bottle must be a pressure gauge. The regulator (to reduce pressure) is next, and that must be followed immediately with an electric solenoid shut-off valve wired to a convenient switch in the cabin, with a bright warning light to tell you when it is on. The fuel line from the solenoid valve to the stove must be continuous—no connections inside the boat except at the stove.

Except when the stove is in use, the solenoid must always be off. When you are through cooking, turn off the solenoid first, then when the burner goes out, turn off the burner. This empties the line of gas so that none will leak into the bilge should a burner valve fail to seal. Once a week turn the burners off first, read the pressure gauge on the tank, then turn off the manual valve. Leave the solenoid valve open. Read the pressure again in 3 minutes and, if unchanged, wait 15 minutes and read it again. Any drop in pressure indicates a leak that must be located (with soapy water) and stopped. If the system is tight, reopen the main valve, light a burner, then shut off the solenoid as normal.

If you'll be the one blown sky-high, take an interest in the proper installation and operation of an onboard LPG stove. An electronic sniffer is a good extra precaution.

Compressed natural gas (CNG) is a safer gas alternative because it is lighter than air, but because of limited availability, CNG isn't a good choice if your cruise will take you outside the United States.

Refrigeration

Refrigeration aboard a boat can either be a joy or the worst headache imaginable. Which it will be depends almost entirely on the installation. You don't have the option of going to your local marine appliance dealer and buying a drop-in unit with a high efficiency rating. A refrigerator on a cruising sailboat is always custom-built, and an inordinate number of new cruisers come to grief here, installing a system that works fine in New England but isn't up to the job south of Mason-Dixon.

Electric refrigeration is the most convenient. Powered by the boat's batteries, electric refrigeration cycles on and off to maintain a set temperature in the box—just like a home refrigerator. The typical installation has a tiny freezer compartment, room enough for a couple of ice trays and maybe a package of frozen chicken. A properly installed system is relatively trouble-free, and other than keeping the batteries charged, electric refrigeration requires little attention.

Mechanical refrigeration is much more powerful, allowing a large freezer in addition to the fridge. Mechanical refrigeration essentially makes a block of 26°F ice (0°F for a freezer) inside a metal container when you run the engine, then the ice keeps the box cold until you run the engine again. An efficient system can operate on as little as 30 minutes of engine running daily, but 1½ to 2 hours of run time is more typical, 4 hours not unheard of. Engine-driven refrigeration is a fairly complicated mechanical system and can be trouble-prone due to that complexity.

Before you conclude that electric refrigeration is the way to go, you should know that a typical installation will use as much as 100 amps of power daily in the tropics, requiring three or four hours of engine time to keep the batteries sufficiently charged.

Whether you have mechanical or electric refrigeration, the key to holding engine time to a tolerable level is the box. The better insulated the box, the more satisfactory the installation. Also a box originally installed to hold 50 to 100 pounds of ice in addition to the food is much too large when converted to refrigeration. Because refrigeration is such a power hog, refrigerate only those things that require it.

Determining a good size isn't difficult. Get a cardboard box about a foot by 2 feet, and maybe a foot deep. Fill it with the items from your home refrigerator you expect to take on the cruise. If they all go in the box, all you need is about 2 cubic feet of refrigerated space; the typical galley ice chest is three to six times that size. Since a "full" refrigerator is the most efficient, the smallest box that will hold what you want to refrigerate is the right size.

If provisions will be your responsibility, you should also determine how well insulated the existing box is. Why? Because if it isn't adequately insulated, you are *not* going to have refrigeration when the boat gets into southern waters, and *you* will be the one most frustrated by that development.

Testing the box is easy. All you have to do is determine how much ice melts in a cold box in 24 hours. Load it with a 25-pound block of ice and let it cool the box overnight. Weigh the remaining ice and add another block, which you also weigh, then leave the box closed for 24 hours. Weigh the ice that remains. If you started with 30 pounds of ice in the precooled box and you have 10 left after 24 hours, 20 pounds melted. It takes 144 Btus to melt a pound of ice, so about 2,880 Btus (20×144) of heat have leaked into the box. Without getting into the math or efficiency assumptions, expect to remove about 3.5 Btus of heat per watt of electrical power; so, offsetting the daily leak into this box will require about 822 watts ($2,880 \div 3.5$), or 68.5 amps in a 12-volt system ($822 \div 12$).

This number might be tolerable except that you haven't cooled anything, haven't opened the lid, and haven't taken into account how much hotter it is where you're headed. The difference between the temperature inside the box, say 40°F, and that outside the box, say 70°F, is called the *differential,* and it is directly related to heat leak. In this example the differential during your test is 30°F, but if the outside temperature is 100°F, the differential will be 60°F and the heat leak will double, meaning the refrigerator will draw 137 amps per day—if it can keep up at all.

Test the box in your galley and pass the results on to the captain. If he is promising refrigeration, the batteries and charging system have to be up to the task. Even mechanical refrigeration with multiple plates will take about an hour to remove 2,880 Btus, so when the thermometer rises into the 90s, you'll be listening to the engine for two hours a day. More than the noise and vibration, it is the obligation that becomes onerous—you *must* be aboard at the appointed hour twice a day to run the engine.

The typical ice-chest conversion fails miserably in the tropics, and many cruisers bitterly revert to buying ice. It is an expensive and frustrating lesson, one you can avoid by simply testing the box. If your test shows excessive energy requirements, believe it.

Having a refrigerator that actually works in the tropics probably involves rebuilding the box. Make it small and well insulated, and make sure the opening has a good double seal and that it is in the top—cold spills out of a front-opening door. It is possible to construct a system that operates almost entirely on wind or solar power, supplemented by the engine on only still or overcast days, but it isn't easy or cheap. A great refrigerator, however, repays the effort well.

In an effort to escape the tyranny of running the engine, cruisers sometimes install propane refrigerators intended for RVs. Because propane refrigerators must sit level to operate, sailors may limit their operation to when the boat is at anchor, but that doesn't address the most serious drawback, namely that when you go ashore, you leave an untended gas flame burning. Propane refrigerators are inherently unsafe inside a sailboat, and no insurer will cover your boat if you install one.

For food preservation there's no substitute for refrigeration, but it isn't required to cool foods and drinks. Try evaporation. Put the bottle or can to be cooled inside a water-soaked sweat sock—seawater is fine—and hang it in the shade. A breeze helps. As the water evaporates, it draws heat from the bottle—the same reason your skin feels cooler when you're wet. This is a simple way to cool wine and soft drinks.

It is ironic to me how often I hear people say, "I wish life was simpler," then without hesitation they add another complication to their lives. Don't try to take all your "modern inconveniences" aboard. The simpler you keep the boat, the sweeter will be the experience.

5

What to Take and Where to Put It

DO YOURSELF A FAVOR AND PARTICIPATE EARLY. YOUR ENTHUSIASTIC PARTNER is thinking about sails and blocks and charts and electronics. Except for agonizing over the right anchors and chain, he probably hasn't given a moment's thought to the day-to-day requirements of living aboard. Someone needs to or your cruise will be far less pleasant than it could be.

Domestic issues usually fall to the mate. Hey, I don't make the news, I just report it. Perhaps you can put off involvement until it is time to step aboard, but the consequent absence of linens, paprika, and bathroom tissue will almost certainly engender regret. It is far better to accept the upcoming cruise as a change in residence—like buying a farm or getting transferred to Borneo—and throw yourself into the move.

A cruise *is* a residence change. If you think of it that way, the things you can do in advance will be obvious.

Clothes

If this were a normal move, *all* your clothes would go with you, but lack of space is almost certain to necessitate some culling. Whether this is a problem depends on your wardrobe. If most of the clothes in your closet are for office dress, leaving those behind may be all you need to do. Some sacrifice! When you aren't at work, if you typically live in favorite sweats or some well-worn jeans and few T-shirts, these can comprise the bulk of your wardrobe aboard—until you reach the land of shorts and swimsuits.

Climate is an issue. If you're headed south, don't take every bulky knit sweater you own; they will ultimately just take up space that you could fill with more useful clothes. On the other hand, don't leave them all behind either. You may need one or two of them before you get beyond the reach of cold weather, and even in the tropics, nights afloat can be cool enough to make a sweater comfortable.

Coats are another space hog. Take a shore coat if you must, but aboard you will be better served by a foul-weather jacket large enough to accommodate several insulating underlayers. The foul-weather jacket shrugs off spray and damp, and you adjust warmth by layering.

Shorts and light shirts will be adequate in warm weather, replaced by jeans and sweatshirts when it is cooler. As the mercury contracts, clothing requirements expand. A suit of thermal underwear will be your most valued possession for cold-weather cruising. When the temperature turns frigid, a third layer of wool or bunting (synthetic fleece) will keep you warm, with foul-weather gear becoming the fourth layer in wet conditions. A warm hat and fleece-lined gloves are essential cold-weather gear.

Regardless of your destination, a sport jacket and the legendary black dress should probably be aboard for the unexpected party or an occasional night out. Also be sure the wardrobe includes slacks for him, skirts for her; not every country is as permissive as the United States, and wearing a bathing suit or shorts ashore in some towns and villages will make you immensely unpopular with the locals.

The fabric may help you decide whether to take a specific item. Don't take anything that isn't washable. Don't take delicates; you probably won't be able to give them proper care. Don't take clothes that aren't relatively wrinkle-free when they line-dry.

Cotton and cotton blends make the best warm-weather fabrics. Cotton is cool and comfortable—just what you want in the tropics—and it ventilates perspiration without picking up odor. However it does get damp and can be less comfortable at night. It doesn't wash well in salt water and can mildew and rot.

Nylon is hot in the daytime, but can be wonderful at night. Clothes made from silklike microfibers are especially effective at shielding from the wind. Since nylon fiber is hydrophobic, that is, it doesn't absorb much water, it is easy to wash. It also dries quickly, which makes it the ideal fabric for swimwear. Avoid nylon underpants, however; they promote urinary infections in a tropical climate.

Polyester is also hot, but is often blended with cotton to yield a fabric less prone to wrinkling and shrinkage. Pure cotton feels better, but away from an iron a polyester blend may look better. Polyester can be combined with *acrylic* into a pile that provides many of the characteristics of wool but dries quickly and never smells like wet sheep. Garments with pile linings make excellent boatwear.

Wool is a warm fabric if you keep it dry, but most ordinary wool garments are absorbent because the fiber's natural grease has been processed out. Heavy Breton-style sweaters of oily wool are extremely warm but perhaps more suitable aboard a fishing boat. Wool socks are good in cold weather; for less harsh conditions choose acrylic or cotton socks.

Cotton thermal underwear is comfortable at first, but the *polypropylene* kind is much better at wicking water away and will keep you comfortable longer. Likewise, polypropylene socks will keep your feet dry longer, and polypropylene gloves are warm but thin enough not to destroy all dexterity.

Color is also a factor. Dark colors are fine in the cold, but when the weather turns hot and sunny, you want light colors. White tops are hard to beat because you can bleach them. Khaki pants and shorts are colorless enough to be cool but more tolerant of stains than white.

Cruising clothes should have a loose fit. In cold weather trapped air keeps you warm, whereas in the tropics loose clothes make you cooler. The restriction of tight clothes is inhibiting when sailing requires quick and/or vigorous action, and loose clothes are simply more comfortable. Leave those skintight jeans at home.

I talk about the sun in a later chapter, but some of your light shirts should have long sleeves. Cool long-sleeve cotton pajamas give good arm and leg protection and are excellent attire for lounging on the boat. Also take scarves and wide-brimmed hats to protect your hair and face.

What about shoes? Despite what our mothers believed, recent scientific studies have confirmed what we should have intuitively concluded all along: no shoes is best for your feet. Where temperatures allow it you can spend most of your time barefoot, but some shoes are required. Deck shoes are a good idea underway, not because they give better footing than bare feet but because they protect your fragile toes from the hazardous landscape. Broken toes are a common—and painful—occurrence among barefoot sailors.

Going barefoot on the beach is fine, but it isn't a good idea in towns and villages where any break in the skin will put you at high risk for picking up an infection. You need comfortable shoes for going ashore, but these shouldn't be your sailing shoes because street wear will destroy their nonskid soles. Thongs (flip-flops) are a common choice, but as town-wear they strike me as sloppy, they offer little protection, and in humid weather you will "skid" on them, risking a turned ankle or worse. If you want to wear sandals ashore, get a pair that buckles onto your foot. Sneakers are probably a better choice, more comfortable for walking distances and providing more protection.

Plan on taking an old pair of sneakers or sandals as "reef shoes" for walking in the shallows or hiking across islands made up of knifelike coral. You will also need the appropriate shoes for your dress outfit(s) for parties and dining out. Limit yourself to one pair, simply because leather shoes aboard a boat require maintenance—periodic airing and sun exposure—or they quickly turn to green suede.

With the possible exception of dress shoes, black soles have no business on a sailboat. They leave ugly marks on fiberglass that are extremely difficult to remove.

Economy dictates starting out with the bulk of your wardrobe aboard, but you will run across many wonderful local fashion items (such as *batiks, molas,* or *sarongs*) along the way. Plan to treat yourself to some of what you see, and save a little space for these acquisitions. Such purchases jazz up your attire on the boat and become unique additions to your wardrobe when you get home.

By the way, the mobile nature of cruising means you are constantly meeting new people, which gives old outfits new life—over and over. A continuing string of compliments can make a few nice outfits ultimately more satisfying than a closet full of clothes ashore.

Don't obsess too much when you are trying to decide between what will be useful and what will be dead weight. A month into the cruise you can box up all the stuff you aren't wearing and for a few bucks send it to your mom's.

Foul-Weather Gear

Staying dry makes the difference between enduring a rainy day and enjoying it, between finding a night watch miserable and finding it magical. A raincoat isn't up to the job; you need good foul-weather gear.

Unless you will be sailing into extreme cold, you need a two-piece suit— thigh-length jacket and bib pants. Although white looks sharp and blues and greens may match your eyes, these are camouflage colors in the ocean. You want yellow, orange, or HERE-I-AM red.

For gear you are counting on to keep you dry, avoid so-called "breath-

able" fabrics. Instead, both jacket and pants should be lined, which insulates you from the condensation that forms inside the waterproof fabric. A slippery lining also makes it easier to get in and out of foul-weather gear.

Good gear has reinforced knees and seat, and crossover suspenders. In the jacket it has both waterproof cargo pockets and insulated slit pockets for keeping hands warm. It includes a good integral hood and reflective tape on the shoulders and elsewhere. Cuffs in both jacket and pants should cinch tight to seal. Zippers should be heavy-duty nylon—including a nylon slide—and protected by double storm flaps. Buy both pieces large enough to fit *loosely* over at least three underlayers.

The best foul-weather gear isn't necessarily the most expensive, but expect a good foul-weather suit to cost around $300 or more. This is no place to cut corners. Cold and discomfort impair the mental processes, often in exactly the circumstances that merit the best judgment. Be sure you have a foul-weather suit capable of keeping you warm and dry in any conditions.

Having said that, I need to point out that offshore gear can be overkill for the lesser demands of coastal cruising where rainy days are spent at anchor and spray is limited to the occasional dollop. Even more to the point, heavy gear can be downright uncomfortable in the tropics. One solution is to buy a "coastal" foul-weather suit, but one heavy enough for occasional offshore use will still be hot for the tropics. A better solution is a lightweight rain suit *in addition to real foul-weather gear.*

A breathable (Gore-Tex or similar) rain suit will be the most comfortable, but even a water-resistant nylon windbreaker will keep you fairly dry. Without lightweight gear, you may be tempted to get wet rather than steam inside a heavy jacket. Or you might just stay below and miss the day entirely. A lightweight suit will keep you from shivering yourself dry after a passing shower, it will give you days you would otherwise write off, it will keep dinghy spray from soaking your shore clothes, and you can stick it in the bottom of your shore bag as bad-weather insurance—not a bad deal for about 50 bucks.

Complete your foul-weather wardrobe with a pair of seaboots. They cost less than a cheap pair of sneakers. Seaboots aren't stylish, but after one watch with wet feet, they will become your most treasured footwear. Seaboots should feel loose; you won't be hiking or line dancing in them. They *must* be large enough to slip out of easily when you have on two pair of socks; otherwise they have the potential to become concrete overshoes.

Linens and Towels

Plan to make up the sleeping bunks on the boat with the same type of bed linens you prefer ashore. Two sets of sheets should be adequate—wash one while using the other. Few boats will have room for a hamper full of dirty sheets. Extra pillowcases, however, can freshen bedding between changes, so take four sets.

One set of guest-bunk sheets will be enough. Even if you have guests back-to-back, you are certain to need to do laundry between (towels, at least). Since guests generally arrive where there is an airport, that also means laundry facilities, or at least a freshwater supply.

Fitted sheets simplify making beds and reduce bottom-sheet bunching. Custom-fitted sheets take less than 20 minutes to sew up on a domestic machine. Start with a flat top sheet large enough to overlap the bunk at least 10 inches all around. A V-berth will take a king-size sheet, and even that may need help by cutting off corners at the foot and sewing them to the sides at the head (see illustration).

Mark the overlapping sheet at the four corners of the bunk, then draw pencil lines from the corner marks perpendicular to the edges of the bunk. The length of the lines will be slightly less than the thickness of the cushion. Extend each of the lines another 4 inches at about 45° to the original and *away from the corner*. Lay the sheet flat and connect the ends of the lines along the sides of the sheet. Trim away the sheet ½ inch outside the pencil line, then hem the straight sides. Now fold the sheet good side to good side to put the two lines at a corner on top of each other and stitch along them from the corner mark to the 45° turn, then on to the hemmed edges. This forms a box at each

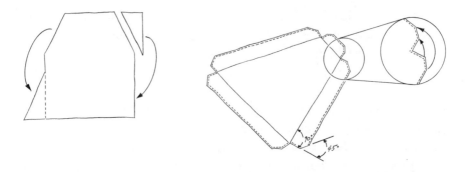

corner of the sheet. Elastic isn't needed; just bend up the corner of the bunk to get it into the formed corner.

On the subject of stitchery, if neither of you sew, enlist the aid of a friend who does. If you cruise for very long, sewing is a skill one of you should polish; after all, the "engine" of your boat is sewn together. A boat also presents opportunities at every turn to make it more attractive, comfortable, and convenient with the simplest sewing projects.

You might like a quilted mattress pad under the bottom sheet; it protects the cushion cover, insulates you from scratchy fabric, pads between-cushion welt cords, and gives the surface extra softness. Buy a regular mattress pad and fit it just like the bottom sheet.

Top sheets should be trimmed to the contour of the bunk, allowing about a foot of overlap all around. Hem the cut edges. Attaching the top sheet to the turned-under portion of the bottom sheet at the foot of the bunk keeps it tucked. Either snaps or Velcro will do the job.

To avoid stripping the bunk in the daytime, consider modifying an attractive comforter into a throw spread. Trim and hem the comforter to the shape of the bunk, about 2 feet longer at the head and overlapping any exposed edges. Pulled down to neck level the comforter will serve its intended function with plenty of overlap at the foot. Pulled up and turned back, it makes an attractive and easy-to-use spread.

Until you run out of space to store them, you can't have too many towels on board. After a few days away from laundry facilities, whether a towel is clean becomes far more important than how big it is. Because you can stow four or five hand towels in the space one bath towel requires, it is usually a good plan to take mostly hand towels. These are plenty absorbent to dry your entire body, and they have the added advantage of drying more quickly. Hand towels also can be hung from lifelines without dragging or doubling.

Nubby towels dry quicker than plush ones. Dark colors dry quicker than light ones. Take a variety of colors to make it easy for everyone to keep up with "their" towel. A couple of beach towels will get plenty of use on and off the boat.

Dishes, Pots, and Utensils

Olga and I haven't used plastic dishes in 20 years, and I can't recall ever breaking or even chipping a dish. You can put aboard whatever kind of dishes you like as long as you also have a custom dishbox to cradle them. To keep dishes from sliding around on the table, cut placemats from waffle-weave nonskid fabric (available in a variety of colors) or run a circular bead of silicone caulk on the bottom of each dish and set it on waxed paper to cure.

If you buy a new set of dishes for the boat, throw away the cups and saucers. Teacups have no use on a boat; you'll scald yourself the first time the boat lurches. Replace them with deep mugs. Resist the temptation to coordinate; a unique mug for everyone avoids a lot of confusion. Most mugs are stoneware, but bone china holds heat better. Use a good china mug just once and it will be your hot-drink choice at home or afloat.

Shallow bowls are also useless except perhaps for salad. You need deep, straight-sided bowls to corral hot liquids. An even better idea for hot soups and the like is to serve them in mugs.

Glassware is less durable than stoneware and china. Crystal isn't a good idea, but some glasswear is tough enough to survive. The problem is that broken glass can be dangerous aboard a boat, and there isn't a clinic down the street to sew you up. Most cruisers opt for acrylic, and if you are headed south, insulated glasses will be appreciated.

Stainless is the only choice for eating utensils. Because you are likely to be dishwashing in salt water, spend a few extra dollars to get good quality stainless. If you are attracted to fancy patterns, keep in mind that a smooth pattern provides fewer nooks and crannies for rust to get a foothold. After a few months the simplest pattern will look the best.

The gadget drawer should include spatulas and spoons, a flat grater (stainless), a whisk, a peeler, a tenderizing hammer (for conch), a hand-crank mixer, and a can opener. Add to that any other items the cook likes, bearing in mind that a sharp kitchen knife and a cutting board will do the same job as various specialty gadgets. Knives, by the way, should be sheathed in a safe holder. Take a ceramic rod to keep the blades sharp.

Cookware can be as little as a skillet, a saucepan, and a kettle, but the cook will appreciate a better selection. A small skillet heats quicker and will be useful when only two are aboard; likewise a small saucepan. Several saucepans will be convenient, and they take up only the space required for the largest. Some cruising cooks use a double boiler to prepare two dishes on one burner.

Every cruising boat should have a pressure cooker aboard. Canning before you leave and along the way can add variety to the cruising menu, but even if you don't do any canning and you've never used a pressure cooker in your life, take one. A pressure cooker cuts cooking time by as much as two-thirds, with an equal reduction in the time the stove is heating the already-hot-enough cabin. That alone earns it a berth, but a pressure cooker does so much more. You can cook any favorite oven casserole in a pressure cooker in one-quarter the time. The pressure tenderizes sometimes-tough local meats. A pressure cooker makes an effective Dutch oven for baking breads, cakes, and custards. If you heat it for about 10 minutes, then put it in an insulated box, it works like a slow cooker. And it is the safest pot to use underway because the lid locks in place. If you don't already own this versatile pot, buy the 6-quart size; the smaller size is too shallow for canning.

Stainless steel pans endure saltwater washing better, but cast aluminum delivers more even heat transfer—particularly important for baking. Cast iron fares poorly in salt water. The new generation of nonstick makes cleaning up a lot easier, especially in tepid seawater. Pot clamps on the galley stove will grip straight-sided saucepans best.

Plastic storage bowls (Tupperware) can do double duty as mixing bowls. You will need a colander, or at least a perforated pot drainer. Institutional-size screw-top plastic jars that restaurants order mayonnaise and other food items in make excellent canisters for dry foods. Ask your neighborhood McDonald's to hold a few for you.

Take at least one thermos bottle. We use a pump thermos mounted in the galley for "running" hot water, but it can also dispense hot coffee or ice water all day. A widemouthed thermos or two is also handy. For example, the easiest way to cook rice is to put a cup of it in a widemouthed thermos, pour in 3 cups of boiling water that has been given a splash of olive oil and ¾ teaspoon of salt, and screw on the lid. It will be ready in about two hours but stays hot and fluffy much longer.

Divide and Conquer

Because boat interiors are square but built into a round hull, there is a lot of hollow space under and behind the furniture, and a well-planned cruising boat gives you access to every inch of it. On a boat it is OK to hide things under the bed and behind the sofa. That's what you're supposed to do.

Boats swallow an amazing amount of gear and equipment, but a few simple modifications will make stowage space more convenient, more secure, and even seemingly larger.

Top-loading lockers are more convenient when the entire top lifts off, rather than a small access hatch. There is a safety concern here; in extreme conditions sailboats have been known to roll beyond horizontal, potentially dumping the entire contents of the locker. This is not something you are likely to risk, but it is easily avoided by latching or screwing the lid down for an off-shore voyage. For the other 95 percent of the time, lifting off the top gives you instant access to everything in the locker.

Compartmentalizing helps top-loading lockers. Fore-and-aft dividers keep small items nearer the top and let you reserve the deepest part of the locker for large items. Athwartship separators tame the jumble of a large locker and make it easier to keep track of where specific items are stowed. Set up as dispenser-like channels, they also provide excellent canned-good stowage.

Without shelves and dividers only the bottom part of front-opening lockers is usable. Shelves allow the use of all the space. You get the most efficient use of the locker if the shelving is spaced to fit the items you keep in the locker. Pot holes are sometimes seen in galley shelves to secure pots, but unless they are cleverly conceived, they waste a great deal of space. Nothing can be stored below the pot shelf because that is where most of the pot ends up, and the space above the shelf also has to be empty to allow the pot to be lifted from its hole. Flat shelves with removable fiddle rails are just as secure and twice as efficient.

Take a cue from refrigerator manufacturers: attach small boxes—either plastic utility boxes from a housewares seller or custom-made wooden ones—to the inside of locker doors to provide extremely convenient stowage for everyday items like sponges, gloves, or dishwashing detergent. Such boxes swing into space that is otherwise unused. Similar boxes attached to the sides of lockers, particularly near the top, can make use of dead space.

Dishes need a secure box that fits the dishes to be contained, even when they will be inside a locker. No design works better than the traditional slot front where dishes are inserted one at a time. An exposed dishbox is convenient, and if it is nicely finished it can be an attractive galley feature. Vertical bins for cutlery are convenient and save drawer space for other galley items.

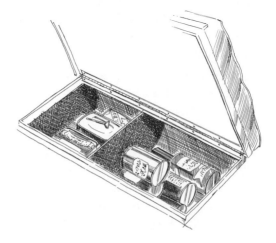

Examine your boat for hidden space. Pulling drawers all the way out often reveals usable space beneath. What is behind the settee back? Extra space can sometimes be made available by simply cutting an access hatch. Is there a way to use the space behind the sink? Could a lift hatch be installed that opens into a suspended trash can or a plywood storage compartment? Open-front boxes let into bulkheads can provide useful storage in the otherwise wasted space in the top of the hanging locker or the forepeak.

Exposed shelves and racks installed on bulkheads and against the hull can be just the ticket for books, CDs, and galley spices. A wide array of manufactured shelves are available, or you can have such shelves custom made. A handy teak rack above your bunk for eyeglasses or near the companionway for sunscreen will be a joy.

A Useful Hanging Locker

If you can't imagine *not* hanging your clothes, consider this. Every time the boat moves, hanging clothes chafe against each other. A few days at sea—whether continuous or in overnight jaunts—can leave your "good" clothes threadbare. It is much like running them in a dryer for days. They will do much better if you fold or roll them.

So what about the hanging locker? The best idea is to convert it to a bureau. For about the price of a similar piece of furniture for your home you can get a boat carpenter to fill the space with drawers. Sometimes a small amount of hanging space for shore clothes—6 to 8 inches—can be reserved behind the drawers and given side access.

Drawers are familiar, convenient, and have the significant advantage of fully containing the clothes. Unfortunately you also need ample space in front of a bureau to pull the drawers out, and more often than not the required space is absent in front of a hanging locker. In this instance shelves will do the same job.

Shelves are slightly less convenient for clothes, but better for towels and linens. They have the advantage of being inexpensive and easy to construct, and they can be taken out for a long stay in port or when you return home. The front 6 inches of the shelves in our hanging locker folds to give us that much hanging space in port.

It is possible to install shelves inside your hanging locker without any carpentry at all. Hem shelf-size panels of acrylic canvas, install grommets in the corners, and lace them tightly to screw eyes installed in the locker. Canvas shelves are perfectly serviceable for soft goods like clothes and linens. If your hanging locker is open, meaning without a door, give your canvas shelves a full-height fiddle by making them long enough for the front to turn up and fasten to or near the shelf above.

Never take wire hangers aboard. They rust. Use plastic hangers, and check them carefully to make sure they are perfectly smooth. Some have mold lines that will chafe or snag your clothes.

The Versatile Canvas Pocket

Canvas has a lot more storage possibilities on a boat. Simply folding a panel in half and sewing up the two sides creates a pocket. Such pockets can be hung against the hull in the back of lockers to keep seldom-used items out of the way, secure, and instantly accessible.

Treated (to resist mildew) natural canvas is much more chafe resistant than acrylic canvas and better for making pockets. Hem the edges or bind them to give the pockets a finished look. A double hem at the top of the back provides tear-resistant reinforcement for attachment. Use snaps in the corners for removable pockets, or install grommets and combine them with cup hooks. Permanent pockets are installed with stainless screws and finishing washers. Hull-side attachment requires fiberglassing a wooden mounting strip in place first.

With a few stitch lines you can divide a large pocket into a number of smaller ones to organize loose items like pot lids and/or plastic-ware lids.

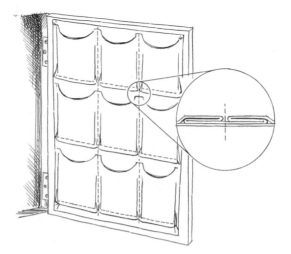

More versatile multipocket bags—like an old-fashioned shoe bag—are easy to construct and can contain more than shoes. Substituting clear vinyl for the front panel of your pockets allows you to see what is inside the pockets and makes them ideal for items like rubber bands, paper clips, and even costume jewelry (don't take the good stuff!).

Obviously Hidden

Despite all the stowage space most boats contain, it probably won't be enough. We almost always start a cruise with a box or two of groceries sitting on an unused bunk. Fortunately (or unfortunately, depending on your point of view) we soon eat our way to a solution.

Unlike food, the volume of clothes, bedding, books, CDs, and such won't shrink as the cruise progresses, so it is important to find room for everything. Some cruisers string net hammocks above bunks to add stowage space, and if they don't offend your aesthetic sense, they are quite effective. A less visible way of accomplishing the same thing is to add elasticized or zippered canvas fronts to above-bunk shelves. This allows such shelves to be packed all the way to the overhead but still look neat. You can also use this same strategy to add stowage *under* a shelf.

Another ploy is to disguise an item. Blankets rolled and stuffed into zippered fabric tubes become bolsters that are attractive additions to a bunk. Similarly, colorful zippered covers let bed pillows spend the daytime on the main salon settee. This also eliminates the need for additional toss pillows.

When preparing for your cruise, take *only* things that will actually get used, then find a place on board for every item. It's as simple as that.

6

Stocking the Galley

THE PROBLEM WITH A CRUISING-BOAT GALLEY ISN'T THE SIZE; A WELL-designed galley is a study in efficiency. Nor is it equipment; there is absolutely nothing you would normally prepare at home you can't do on the boat. The problem with the cruising-boat galley is location.

It isn't near a supermarket.

When you grocery shop at home, you buy a single head of lettuce, maybe three or four lemons, one carton of eggs—only enough perishables to accommodate your immediate needs. You likely limit your nonperishable purchases as well; why keep more than a couple of cans of tomato paste on hand when you're restocking every week? Preparations for "special" meals are almost certainly to begin with a run to the market anyway.

We tend to treat supermarkets as a kind of super pantry. It isn't quite as convenient as a well-stocked cupboard, but we don't have to invest it with forethought, and it is sure to have everything we need. Cruising requires a different mind-set.

In the quaint places of the world favored by cruisers, grocery stores are routinely little more than a couple of shelves of dusty canned goods, a bin of local produce, and maybe a rust-pocked freezer with a few frozen items of questionable pedigree. At cruising pace, ports boasting well-stocked markets can be weeks apart. When you reach one, the market can be far from the waterfront, and its prices can devastate a cruising budget.

The solution is to stock the boat as fully as possible before you leave. Cruising boats larger than 30 feet will have little difficulty hiding away a three- or four-month food supply. A fully stocked boat lets you limit food purchases to just produce and local bargains until you reach a good supply port.

It is worth pointing out that going cruising relieves you of the weekly drudgery of grocery shopping and reintroduces you to the convenience of having everything you need on hand. Most find cruising puts the joy back in food shopping; market forays become associated with special treats rather than being just a recurring and expensive chore, and unfamiliar stores, especially in foreign countries, are filled with interesting and exotic products.

Of course you can't take aboard a four-month supply of produce. Well, that's not entirely true; stored properly, some fresh items keep for a surprisingly long time. But it would be disingenuous not to admit that keeping the galley supplied with fresh fruits and vegetables is a challenge—or a pain—depending mostly on your attitude. If you have to have lettuce and tomatoes, you are in for considerable frustration. But if you are willing to substitute cabbage, indulge in 25-cent pineapples, seek out eggplant recipes, and give mamey a try, you could find the produce hunt one of your cruise's best features.

If you are a meat-eater and your boat is not equipped with a dependable freezer, cruising will change your diet. Of course you are almost certain to find yourself substituting fresh—and I do mean fresh—seafood. Considering the relative health merits of fish versus beef, it is hard to think of this as a particularly bad thing. You won't have to give up meat altogether. Fresh meat will be available along the way—one of the aforementioned "special treats." And both canned and dried meats can more than adequately satisfy the requirements of many main-dish recipes.

Exactly what you take aboard is a matter of taste—literally—but the following sections will help you with the process and perhaps introduce you to some new culinary possibilities.

The Shopping List

Shopping successfully for three or four months requires a comprehensive shopping list. You should take the first step toward developing such a list at least a month, and preferably three, before the cruise.

With a felt-tip marker, go through your refrigerator and cabinets and mark the level of *all* your condiments, cooking supplies, and paper products. After exactly a month, recheck the levels and note your consumption on a list. If, for example, your pint of white vinegar was half empty when you marked the label and now it is three-quarters empty, your monthly consumption is about 4 ounces.

When you use up the contents of a marked container during the test, saving the empty usually requires less effort than making an interim notation. At the end of the month just add the volume of the empty container(s) to what is missing from the active one to get total monthly consumption. In other words, if you end the month with an unmarked pint bottle of vinegar half empty, and two vinegar bottles are among your saved empties, one the half-full marked original, your monthly consumption is about 32 ounces.

This strategy lets you get a quick handle on how much sugar, flour, oil, ketchup, mustard, aluminum foil, etc. you typically use in a month. Translate this to your shopping list by multiplying it times the number of months you are shopping for. In the case of essential condiments, buying for the full anticipated duration of the cruise can be a good idea if the volume is manageable.

Of the various ways of estimating food requirements, the most satisfactory is to prepare menus. Breakfast is the easiest because it typically has the least variety. If both of you are cereal-eaters, just monitor your cereal and milk consumption for a month as part of your condiment survey. If breakfast every day is half a grapefruit, a slice of toast, and a cup of coffee, you need 3½ grapefruit and 7 slices of bread—about ⅓ of a loaf—per week per person. Buying for two people for 3 months (13 weeks), you would need 91 grapefruit and about 9 loaves of bread. Of course, neither grapefruit nor bread will keep for 3 months. You might take aboard about 20 grapefruit—enough to last 3 weeks—but packaged bread will be stale in less than a week. You can often buy bread locally, and perhaps fruit, too, but for stocking purposes you need to find a grapefruit substitute for 10 weeks (probably canned or dehydrated juice) and increase your stock of flour and milk enough to bake 8 loaves of bread *for breakfast*. Appropriate amounts of jelly, butter, coffee, sugar, and even creamer should already be on your list from your condiment survey.

In reality breakfast tends to have more variety aboard than ashore, probably because time is available to enjoy breakfast, but also because variety takes on new importance on a boat. Maybe you would like to have bacon and eggs once or twice a week, and an occasional omelet. You might prefer muffins, biscuits, or pancakes rather than toast. Grits and hash browns are easy enough to prepare on a boat. And, oh, corned-beef hash; it's s-o-o-o good.

Plan your breakfast menu for 2 weeks: cereal 3 days, eggs and bacon 3 days, muffins twice, pancakes twice, biscuits and grits twice, omelet and hash browns once, and corned-beef hash once. Break each breakfast down into ingredient amounts, i.e., 2 bowls (about 4 ounces) of cereal and 8 ounces of milk; 2 eggs, 4 slices of bacon, 2 slices of bread (toast), and 12 ounces of orange juice; ½ box of blueberry muffin mix; etc. Multiply daily amounts times the number of times that breakfast is included in the 2-week menu, then multiply that times 6.5 to get your 3-month requirement.

A heartier breakfast usually results in a lighter lunch—soups when it is cool, sandwiches and cheeses in hot weather. Fourteen lunch menus will mean they repeat only once a month, but don't include things you don't like just to increase variety; it is better to take more of something you like. As with breakfast items, once you decide you want 1 package of chicken-noodle soup or 2 small cans of tuna every 2 weeks, it is easy enough to calculate the 3-month requirement. Olga and I always reduce our lunch list by about 25 percent to take into account dinner leftovers, lunches ashore, and the appetite-depleting affects of midday tropical heat.

Dinner requirements are the hardest to anticipate. You will be happier with the variety if you expand the menu plan to four weeks, but rather than work out each day's menu, just plan the main course. Throw in a few open days for sampling local eateries, for the fresh items you are likely to snatch up at every opportunity, and for seafood you hook, spear, or pick up.

Now plan two side dishes for each day. They need not correspond with the main courses; you just want to have enough vegetable and fruit "values" to prepare well-rounded meals. We use a lot of rice, especially with seafood, and reduce our side dish total appropriately.

If a meal to you isn't complete without dessert, work out a two- or four-week dessert plan and add ingredients to your list that aren't already part of your condiment survey.

Snacks are an essential part of cruising, whether you are entertaining or simply satisfying midafternoon munchies. Make a list of things you like—nuts, dried fruits, popcorn, crackers, chocolate—and include a generous supply of each on your list. I've never met a single cruiser who felt he or she had brought too many snack items aboard.

By now you have a fairly complete list. You still have to decide about beer, wine, and soft drinks. The quantity of these items is most often determined by how much stowage space, if any, remains after everything else is aboard.

Wine, by the way, ages quickly with the motion of the boat. Inexpensive young wines will taste quite mature in a couple of months. Reds cruise better and don't need chilling. You can safely store wines upright; the motion will keep corks moist.

If you doubt that everything on your list will fit aboard, do your shopping in phases. Buy only one-month's supplies on the first trip. Once these are well stowed, you will have a good feel for whether there is barely room for a second month or the lockers can swallow up three more months' worth.

Fresh Foods

Fresh foods will actually be the last items you put aboard, but their availability influences your selection of preserved alternatives.

Fruits and vegetables generally don't require refrigeration, but there are preparation and stowage procedures that can significantly extend shelf life. All benefit from being cool, but some also need to be moist while others need to be dry. Some do better out in the open; others last longer kept in the dark.

You can extend the life of all fresh fruits and vegetables by "sterilizing" their outer surfaces. Add 1 tablespoon of *plain* chlorine bleach (Clorox) to 2 gallons of water and soak the fresh produce for about 30 minutes. Pat the produce with a clean (and preferably bleached) towel and place it in the sun on another clean towel for about an hour to thoroughly dry. The chlorine completely dissipates in the air and sunlight. By the way, never bring aboard the packing produce comes in; it often harbors roaches and other critters, and it adds to your trash-disposal problem.

Store sterilized produce in a single layer in shallow boxes or baskets that have first been scrubbed with a strong bleach solution and allowed to dry. Custom storage trays are easily constructed by stapling fiberglass screening to knocked-together wood frames. Lockers below the waterline and against the hull will be about the same temperature as the outside water, making them the coolest spots in a boat in subtropical or tropical waters and a good place to store produce. Lockers used for produce stowage must be well ventilated.

Here are specific instructions for storing a number of common vegetables and fruits after you sterilize and dry them:

Apples—Select small, firm apples. Wrap individually in tissue paper and store in the dark. If they are packed so they don't bruise, apples will last up to two months. Check weekly and cut away bruises, rubbing the spot with lemon juice. Use bruised apples first.

Apricots—Apricots should be firm but not green. Individually wrapped in tissue, they will last about a week.

Avocados—Wrapped separately in tissue paper, bruise-free avocados will last three weeks. Unwrap and set out to ripen.

Bananas—Green bananas will last a couple of weeks if they are stored in the dark. Unless you want spiders aboard, submerge all stalks of bananas for three minutes before you bring them aboard. Dipping them in the sea is fine for ripening bananas, but bananas you plan to store should be dipped in fresh water only.

Bell peppers—Green, yellow, and red bell peppers will last about 10 days stored in a cool spot.

Berries—Forget about storing berries. Put them out and eat them while they are in their prime.

Broccoli—Broccoli will keep about two weeks wrapped in a sterile cloth and spritzed daily with chlorinated water. Or store for a week by hanging it upside down by the stem.

Cabbage—Soak cabbage longer in the sterilizing dip (about two hours—agitating the head occasionally). Stored in a cool, ventilated locker, cabbage will keep two to three weeks. Cloth-wrapped heads spritzed daily with chlorinated water—½ *teaspoon* of bleach to 1 gallon of water—will keep four to five weeks if you wipe the head and change the cloth every few days. Trim the stalk if it gets soft or black.

Carrots—"Planted" in a box of moist sand, fresh carrots and other root vegetables will keep a month or longer. Leave the roots on, trim foliage to 1 inch, and store the box in a cool spot. Packaged carrots won't keep well without refrigeration.

Cauliflower—Select cauliflower that is white, without any yellow tinge. It will keep about two weeks wrapped in a sterile cloth and spritzed daily with chlorinated water. Or store for a week by hanging it by the stem.

Celery—Even wrapped in a wet cloth, celery goes limp in about three days. If you want fresh celery, refrigerate it.

Citrus—Use double the chlorine content of your spritzing water, 1 teaspoon rather than ½ to a gallon of water, to wipe the skin of citrus weekly to prevent mold. Grapefruit, oranges, and tangerines suspended in a mesh bag in a cool, dark location will last four to six weeks.

Coconut—Husk brown coconuts and store the nut in a dry location. They can last for months and make a great snack food.

Corn—On the cob, corn will last about 10 days wrapped in cloth and spritzed daily with chlorinated water.

Cucumbers—Buy cucumbers dark green. Store them in a cool, low-light location and turn them twice a week. They last about two weeks.

Garlic—Hang garlic and keep it dry. It will last two months or longer.

Green beans—After a week green beans become tough and will be inferior to the canned variety.

Lemons—Buy lemons slightly green. Individually wrapped in foil and stored in an airtight container, lemons last almost forever. Limes can be stored the same way.

Lettuce—Wrap lettuce in sterile cloth and spritz it daily with chlorinated water. Iceberg and romaine will last up to 10 days in a temperate climate, half that in the tropics.

Melons—Keep cool. Cantaloupe and honeydew must generally be consumed within a week. Small watermelons stored with good air circulation can last up to a month.

Onions—Onions last longer stored in the dark, up to eight weeks, but tend to sprout. Keep sprouts pared off. Suspend onions in a mesh bag for good air circulation.

Peaches—Purchased rock hard and wrapped individually in tissue, peaches will last about a week. Green peaches may fail to ripen.

Pears—Wrap in tissue paper and store in the dark. Bring out to ripen. Pears purchased hard and green can last up to two weeks.

Pineapples—Purchased green, pineapples will keep up to three weeks. Store upright in a cool location.

Potatoes—Store potatoes in the dark, but not with your onions, which steal moisture from them. Cool, dry potatoes will keep six weeks or longer, but check regularly to remove eyes and to cull any showing spoilage. New potatoes keep the best.

Radishes—Radishes will keep about two weeks submerged in chlorinated water.

Squash—Acorn, pumpkin, and butternut squash require no special care and will last up to six weeks.

Tomatoes—Buy tomatoes green, just starting to blush. Wrap them individually in tissue paper and store inside a cool locker. They will last six to eight weeks. Set out (but not in *direct* sunlight) two days before use.

Zucchini—Wiped daily with a paper towel dampened with chlorinated water, zucchini will last about 10 days.

Eggs don't need to be refrigerated, but they do need to be sealed. The traditional method is to completely coat each egg with Vaseline to seal the shell outside. An easier method is to put the eggs in a wire basket and lower them into boiling water for exactly 10 seconds, which seals the shell from the inside.

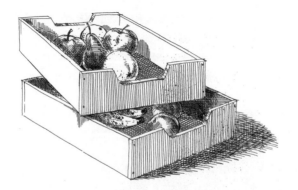

Eggs will keep for about a month without any assistance. If you turn the cartons over twice a week to keep the "top" of the shell from drying out inside, untreated eggs will keep two months or longer.

The yolk membrane degenerates as eggs age, so don't be surprised if your eggs reach a point where the yolks always break. Unless the egg is discolored or smells bad, it is still perfectly good. Check eggs by putting them into a glass of water; if they float, they are rotten. It is a good idea to crack older eggs into a cup rather than directly into your recipe.

Fresh meats should never be kept at room temperature. Meats must be immediately cooked, refrigerated, frozen, or otherwise preserved.

Canned Foods

It is tempting to turn up your nose at canned foods as inferior to fresh, but that's much like saying the southern way of slow cooking green beans is inferior to the quick-steam haute cuisine method. Don't be so sure unless you've tried both ways.

It is certainly true that some canned foods are awful, but others can provide the basis for dishes that rival those prepared from fresh ingredients. The trick is to find canned foods you like and recipes that enhance them. Lin Pardey, the cruising nation's best ambassador, recommends "can night," a once-a-week meal made up entirely of canned or packaged foods. This provides the opportunity in the months before your departure to identify canned foods you like and eliminate those you don't.

Some canned vegetables are good right out of the can, but more often they are bland and need the addition of onions, peppers, salt, or other flavor enhancers. Buy yourself a cookbook that features canned ingredients; plenty of them are available.

If your cruise takes you into hot weather, canned fruits become more appealing than vegetables. This mostly has to do with the fact that the fruits are served cool or even chilled. Chilled vegetable dishes like bean salads and relishes also become more popular. Keep this in mind when you are working up your supply list.

A word of caution; some canned items, especially some hams, require refrigeration. Read the label. You take an awful risk if you store these unrefrigerated.

There is little useful I can offer further on canned goods except to say Keep your eyes open. Supermarkets carry a staggering array of canned foods, many of which you may have passed right by for years without noticing. Drug and discount stores often have an aisle or two of specialty foods, some of which may merit your attention. For example, Kmart stores sometimes stock a canned bacon that keeps for months without refrigeration, and Walgreens often feature at a good price canned shrimp that can become the key ingredient in a delicious sandwich spread.

Canning Your Own

If the idea of home canning sounds too retro, exactly the kind of backward step this whole cruising enterprise represents to you, take it easy. Although canning opens new culinary avenues, not unlike, say, the purchase of a bread-maker, we are going to limit ourselves to the basics—little more than storing food in sterile jars.

Forget about canning fruits and vegetables unless you grow your own. Commercial products will be easier, cheaper, and probably better. Where home canning is worth the effort is for the preservation of meats. Home-canned beef will be as good as or better than fresh for almost any use except grilling.

A supply of canned beef, both chunks and ground, facilitates a wide variety of menu possibilities. The meat is tenderized in the canning process, so you can select cheaper cuts, but they should be lean and boneless. Cut solid beef into pieces that will pack conveniently into your jar.

What size jars should you use? A pint jar holds about a pound of meat, which is probably the most convenient size for families or for two people with hardy appetites. If your tastes run to lighter fare, you might prefer ½-pint jars. Check what your recipes call for.

The canning process is uncomplicated. Wash and rinse the jars, then fill them with hot water until you need them. The meat can be either browned slightly or raw-packed. Empty the water and immediately fill the hot jars with the meat, leaving at least 1 inch of "head space" at the top. Cover the meat entirely with hot water or broth, working out bubbles with a clean spatula and still leaving 1 inch at the top. Wipe the rims clean, put on a new lid, and screw on the screw band. Follow the lid manufacturer's directions for how tight.

Put the cooking rack in the bottom of your pressure cooker, pour in 5 cups of water, then place the packed jars on the rack. A 6-quart cooker usually holds four 1-pint jars. Lock the lid in place, put on high heat, and after the vent steams for 5 minutes, install the pressure valve, reduce the heat, and keep the valve rocking gently for the specified processing time—1 hour for beef, 40 minutes for chicken at 15 pounds pressure. That's it. Let everything cool naturally, check the seal on the jars, and put them away until it is time to make spaghetti bolognese or beef burgundy.

If most of your ground-beef recipes call for onions, peppers, and tomato paste, you can avoid using your limited fresh supplies later by mixing these into the meat before you can it.

Canned chicken is available commercially, but you might try canning your own for comparison. If they taste the same to you, or the store brand is better, put your canning efforts into something else. Regardless of who does the canning, the process robs chicken of some of its flavor. Compensate by adding a bit of bouillon to your recipes.

Can pork just like beef. Prefrying sausage into patties before you pack it will give you long-life "brown-and-serve" sausage. You can pack beef patties the same way for *Grilled Burgers à Paradise.*

With an inexpensive supply of new lids aboard, it is easy enough to restock along the way. When the sea is generous, you can preserve excess fish by canning it, but canned fish tends to fall apart, making it mostly useful for chowder.

If you process the meat correctly it will be as safe as cans off the shelf. You will probably never have a jar go bad, but should the seal fail or the contents have an off smell, throw it out without tasting. As a safeguard you can make a habit of emptying canned meats into your pressure cooker and bringing it up to full pressure before you use them. If you have any doubts— the food doesn't look or smell right—discard it.

Slip each canning jar into an old but clean tube sock before you pack it into the boat's lockers. All bottles and jars can be protected from breakage this way.

Dehydrated Foods

A number of dehydrated foods are available in the supermarket. Beans, boxed potatoes, raisins, and beef jerky are four that come immediately to mind. Dehydrated foods are compact, lightweight, and almost immune to spoilage as long as they remain dry, which makes them ideal for the cruising galley. Their only drawback is that rehydrating requires water. (Tip: Some dried foods are improved by rehydrating in milk, juice, even wine.)

You need not be limited to the dried items on the supermarket shelf. Home dehydrators aren't expensive, and most fruits, vegetables, and meats can be preserved by drying. A dehydrator is probably a worthwhile investment in your cruise just for the inexpensive and nutritious snack foods it can turn out. Check with friends before you buy one; you might find one you can borrow.

Don't confuse dehydrating with freeze-drying. Although freeze-dried foods can be excellent, they tend to be expensive. Their biggest drawbacks for the cruising galley is that they aren't compact, requiring the same space as canned equivalents, and they use lots of water in preparation. Freeze-drying requires special equipment not found in the typical home kitchen.

Dehydrating, in contrast, has to be the easiest of all preservation methods. Put a single layer of the food in the dehydrator tray and turn the machine on. In a few hours the food is dry and ready to be stored in an airtight container. The food item might be dried whole or sliced, depending on what it is.

What might you dehydrate? Fruits such as apples, apricots, bananas, and pineapples dry well and make great snack foods. They also substitute perfectly for fresh fruits in most baking recipes. You can buy dried fruits, but the home-dried variety are almost always superior.

You can dry almost any vegetable. A supply of dried carrots, celery, corn, mushrooms, peppers, and squash will substitute, often indiscernibly, for the fresh vegetables many recipes specify. Cooked, dried spinach is indistinguishable from fresh. Dried slices of zucchini, carrots, or cucumbers make interesting happy-hour chips.

Meats dry into jerky—tough, chewy strips that many people love and an equal number hate. Jerky is essentially a high-protein snack food, and home-dehydrated jerky shouldn't be kept unrefrigerated more than one month. Rehydrated jerky can be used in soups and stews and even stir-fried, but canned meat is generally better suited.

Fruit leathers are one of the best dehydrator products. This is nothing more than a fruit purée—like applesauce—with the water removed. You probably know fruit leathers as "fruit roll-ups." As good as commercial fruit roll-ups are, you can make better ones, and in any flavor you like. Aside from its undeniable snack value, fruit leather also makes a great base for quick jam or for juice drinks. This is how to have orange juice for breakfast long after the oranges are exhausted.

Tomatoes merit special mention. Sun-dried tomatoes are today enjoying great popularity in culinary circles, recognition they surely deserve. Dried tomatoes are a wonderful galley item but quite expensive. With a few pounds of Roma tomatoes and a dehydrator you can have sufficient dried tomatoes to give away some, which will make you very popular. Pulverize some of your dried tomatoes into a powder in your blender and you have a compact supply of tomato sauce and tomato paste—just add water.

Speaking of sun-drying, you can dry foods without an electric dehy-drator—our ancestors did it for centuries—but it is harder to get consistent results. Getting foods to dry in the humid marine environment can be par-ticularly challenging. If you experiment with sun-drying during your cruise, try using a framed screen suspended below the forehatch with the windscoop rigged. Fruit leathers can be dried on plastic wrap in direct sunlight. Drying meats will require about three days of clear sunlight, with the meat in a clear plastic bag propped open to the wind and wiped dry every 30 minutes on the last day. Bring drying foods in at night.

Grow Your Own

Growing sprouts is a delicious way to have fresh vegetables no matter how far from a market you are. Sprouts add a wonderful fresh taste and crunch to sandwiches, salads, and stir fry, to name just a few uses. If you don't like sprouts, maybe you just haven't tried the right ones. Health-food stores (and some supermarkets) carry dozens of different seed varieties.

Sprouting is easy. The only equipment you need is a clean, widemouthed quart jar. Put about 2 tablespoons of seeds in the jar, then cover the mouth with cheesecloth or flexible screening held on with a rubber band. Pour ½ cup of water over the seeds and let them soak to soften the seed coat.

After 12 hours pour off the water; the cheesecloth keeps the seeds in the jar. Rinse the seeds in fresh water and drain it off. Lay the jar on its side with the seeds evenly distributed, then prop up the bottom to give the seeds good drainage. Keep your little garden in a cool, *dark* place; light will turn the sprouts green and can make them bitter and tough.

Here's the hard part about farming. You have to rinse the sprouts at least twice a day, but in two to three days you'll have a crop ready to harvest. Take what you need and keep up your daily rinsing. Sprouts will continue to grow for about a week. If you haven't eaten them by then, they will keep for another week refrigerated in a sealed plastic bag, longer if you rinse them occasionally.

Stocking requires no more than putting aboard a variety of seeds. Get a few samples from a helpful health-food store and sprout them at home to find what you like. Alfalfa and mung bean are the mainstays, but try radish and Chinese cabbage. Mixing seeds will give you a blend of flavors.

Spices

Many spices lose potency with time. Going cruising is a perfect opportunity to start fresh with the spices you will most use. Buy spices in screw-top containers, and stow them away from the heat of the galley stove.

If you have a dehydrator, you might try drying fresh herbs you normally use at home. Herbs should be dried at low temperature—about 100°F. To add native herbs to your spice rack, suspend them inside a paper bag to dry, then put them in an airtight container. When substituting dried herbs for fresh, use about a quarter of the called-for amount.

Wahoo—and Other Seafood to Shout About

Olga and I have occasionally encountered new cruisers who set out with little more than bag of rice and a supply of tartar sauce. Perhaps they imagined fish would just leap into their boat. It doesn't work like that.

Many popular cruising destinations were long ago "fished out." Others are protected, with fishing limited or prohibited entirely. Waters near population centers can be so foul you wouldn't consider eating anything living in them. Even where the water is pristine and loaded with delicacies, getting them takes effort. And as any fisherman knows, sometimes they just "ain't bite'n."

Before you count on the bounty of the deep for more than the occasional meal, you need to decide how much of your cruising time you will be willing to spend catching dinner. We eat a lot of seafood when we cruise, but we cruise in warm waters and we love to dive. We spear most of the fish we eat, and we pick up conch and lobster off the bottom. Occasionally something stupid snags itself on our fishing line—which is great fun—but if we had to catch fish to eat, we'd end up awfully hungry.

The best stocking strategy is not to count on seafood, no matter how confident your partner is about this. If it turns out to be plentiful, your supplies merely last longer.

Goat Meat, Mon

If you cruise outside the United States, many of the countries you visit, maybe all of them, will have U.S.-style supermarkets. Canned and packaged items will be similar to or the same as those your store at home carries—except for the price. Produce is likely to be mostly local, and what you see is what you get. The big unknown is meat.

The issue is not so much about whether the meat will be safe, although I do recall hearing about a meat vendor in Mexico who kept his hanging carcasses free of flies by spraying the meat with Raid. Such horror stories aside, the real issue is whether the meat will be edible.

We generally buy grain-fed beef in America, couch-potato cows that get fat and soft on their way to the slaughterhouse. A cow's life in many foreign countries isn't as easy, and range cattle tend to be tough and have a different taste. Beef in poorer countries may well be suitable only for stewing. Always sample before you buy in quantity.

Pork is less risky—pigs everywhere are fat and lazy. Trichinosis is not a problem as long as you cook the pork well; cooked pork should be white, never pink.

Goat and lamb are more available than beef and pork in many places. Both are fine stew meats. Marinated on ice or in the refrigerator for 24 hours in oil, vinegar, white wine, and seasoning, both lamb and goat make wonderful shish kebab, sufficient reason to take a package of wooden skewers. Ground lamb or goat can substitute for ground beef in most recipes.

Chickens also have a tougher life in hardscrabble places. The younger the chicken, the tenderer it will be, so don't buy the biggest chicken in the case.

If it looks and smells fresh, meat purchased in foreign markets is no more likely to pose serious health risks than what you buy at home. If you can get meat past your nose, your stomach can handle it. Surface bacteria will be destroyed in the cooking process. Because grinding distributes these bacteria throughout the meat, it is imperative to cook ground beef well done, to at least 155°F. If the interior is still pink, it isn't done enough.

Keeping Track

With a three-month supply of food aboard, finding the canned asparagus can be a problem. Here are some methods of keeping track.

The master notebook. List all the supplies aboard—preferably in alphabetical order. Give each cabinet or locker a numerical designation—written on the locker and shown on a map in the notebook—then place a notation beside each entry to indicate the cabinet or locker you stowed that item in.

The chart. On a large sheet of paper sketch the boats interior, then pencil each item in its location right on the chart. A derivative method is to number the lockers, give corresponding numbers to pages in a notebook, and write in each item on the appropriate page.

Dedicated lockers. This is the easy way. Use one locker for fruits, one for vegetables, etc. Looking for corned beef? It's in the meat locker; no book to consult, no chart to check.

A reality of stowage lockers is that some are more accessible than others. A good stowage plan makes the best use of the most accessible lockers. If your menu plan calls for ham only once or twice a month, don't put eight hams in your most convenient locker. Besides filling it up, you'll have to move all those hams aside each day in your quest for chicken or beef. Stow just two there and send all the others to "cellar" storage in harder to access lockers. Go into the cellar(s) once a month to restock the convenient lockers.

Some cruisers maintain an inventory, writing down each item used so they know what needs to be transferred into the "daily" lockers, and ultimately what they need to buy. Again, Olga and I take the easy way. We restock by getting a couple of everything from the cellar, more of high-use items like tomato sauce. If we end up with too much of something in the daily locker, we send it back to the cellar.

As for shopping, an item gets on our list when we take the last one out of the cellar. If we find ourselves with an opportunity to do major replenishing, we almost always inventory all the lockers, preferring this to keeping lists.

One final tip: If your can storage is upright, write the contents of each can on its top with a waterproof marker. Two- or three-letter shorthand will be adequate. This lets you tell the corn (CRN) from the green beans (GRB) without having to lift cans to see the labels.

7

Underway

I WOULDN'T ARGUE WITH ANYONE WHO POINTED OUT THAT KNOWING HOW to handle the boat is more important than the stain resistance of khaki or the amount of cooking oil aboard. However, for the reluctant cruiser, what to take is almost always confronted before "driving" the boat, so that is the sequence chosen for this book.

If you are already a skilled sailor, this chapter isn't for you. If your partner is the sailor, read on.

It is tempting to think that other cruisers must know a lot more about boats than you do, but you would be wrong. A lot of cruisers, women espe-

cially, start their cruise with little if any boathandling experience. They leave all boat handling to someone else, participating only with direction—"release that line" or "turn the wheel to the right." Reluctant cruisers are particularly likely to avoid boat issues before departure. Only as the cruise progresses do they acquire boathandling skills.

Some dragged-aboard cruisers learn the ropes quickly and within days are competent if not enthusiastic sailors. Others find unexpected fulfillment at being in control and soon enough share or usurp the captain's responsibilities. A few go through the entire cruise without ever having a clue.

Don't let yourself slide into this last group. Despite the long odds against your cruising partner becoming incapacitated, it can happen. Being able to deal with that possibility can keep an "incident" from becoming a disaster, and knowing you can deal with it relieves you of one of your greatest worries.

You can quell this concern even earlier by learning to handle your boat before you leave, a course I strongly recommend; but even if you don't do that, you should be able to pick up all the essentials in the first couple of days of your cruise. Providing a good environment for learning the basics is one of the reasons it is so important that the early days of a cruise proceed at a relaxed pace.

Powering

Learn first how to start the engine. This is usually no more involved than starting a car—simply turn a key or push a button—but some boat engines exhibit starting quirks, especially when they are cold. Don't just watch. *You* turn the battery selector to the correct position. *You* check to see that the stop control is in. *You* make sure the prop is disengaged. *You* start the engine.

Find out if there is a "cold-start" button on the engine or the control panel and when you need to activate it. Is there a valve in the exhaust line that needs to be opened or a lock on the prop shaft that needs to be released? Make starting the engine your job the first few days of the cruise. The time may come when your ability to start the engine instantly, without needing to think about it, can avert disaster.

Engaging the propeller is equivalent to putting an automatic-transmission car in gear, only more intuitive. Push the shift lever forward to go forward; pull it back to back up. As with your car, you don't want the engine racing when you put it in gear, so be sure the throttle is at idle—its lowest setting—before you move the shift lever. When you shift into forward or reverse, push the shift lever as far as it will go. When the lever is in the middle position, usually upright, you are in neutral—out of gear.

The throttle is most often a second lever you push forward to make the engine run faster and pull back to slow down, but on some boats it is a T-handled plunger-type control that you pull out to accelerate. A few sailboats use a single-lever dual-function control that both engages the transmission and accelerates the engine when you push (forward) or pull (reverse) the single lever, but dual-function controls are far more common on powerboats.

So far, driving a boat isn't much different from driving a car—start the engine, put it in gear, and give it the gas. But what about steering? If your boat has a tiller, it will seem backward to you the first time you take the helm. When you move the tiller to the right, you expect the boat to go to the right, but it goes left. This is because boats steer from the back—where the rudder is. When you move the tiller to the right, it is the back of the boat that goes right, which makes the bow of the boat turn to the left. As confusing as this is at first, after an hour or two on the tiller your brain will correct its erroneous assumption, and tiller movements will become automatic.

Wheel steering is almost like driving your car—move the top of the wheel to the right and the boat turns right. I say "almost" because the boat still steers from the back, so while the boat turns to the right, the stern actually moves to the left. This is of no consequence in open water, but it means you can't pull a boat away from the dock like you pull a car away from the curb.

The biggest difference between driving a car and driving a boat is that boats have no brakes. Fortunately boats tend to stop when you disengage the propeller. How quickly depends on how heavy the boat is. A supertanker moving at top speed, for example, might take 3 miles to come to a complete stop, while a planing inflatable dinghy stops so fast it almost pitches you over the bow when you suddenly stop the engine. A cruising sailboat typically carries on for several boat lengths when you disengage the prop (or drop sails). If that will be too far, you put on the brakes by putting the engine in reverse. This doesn't bring the boat to a screeching halt, but panic stops are rarely called for. If you are moving slowly and you "play" the throttle in reverse, you will be able to stop the boat exactly where you want it.

Backing a sailboat is like parallel parking, both in how difficult and how essential it is. Back your boat cleanly into a slip and you will garner admiration from everyone who sees you do it, but having this skill isn't fundamental to your safety. That doesn't mean you shouldn't eventually learn this aspect of boat handling.

You learn to drive a boat the same way you learn to drive a car—by doing it. Start the first day, and don't just steer. Speed up. Slow down. Turn. Circle. Throw a cushion in the water and learn to stop right beside it. It doesn't take long to gain confidence, and the knowledge that if you have to you can get "in" without assistance is quite reassuring.

Sailing

If you are a total novice to sailing, on the very first day of your cruise learn to turn the boat into the wind and take the sails down. Dealing with an emergency will be easier for you under power.

Always drop the forwardmost sails first. "Take off" a roller-furling sail by releasing the sheets and pulling on the furling line. This is usually easy but can require more force in heavy winds. If you aren't strong enough, put the furling line around a cockpit winch and crank it in with the handle.

Hank-on headsails and those on the mast(s), like the mainsail and the mizzen, come down by simply releasing the halyard and pulling the sail down. The "tail" of the halyard should be tied. If it isn't, don't turn it loose or it will run right up to the top of the mast. Secure dropped sails with sail ties or a piece of line, and make absolutely sure no lines are dangling over the side where they can become entangled in the propeller.

If all this sounds like it takes time, you're right. In a man-overboard situation, for example, you can almost always return to the spot much more quickly under sail. That alone is reason enough to learn to handle your boat under sail.

Sailor or not, you will soon find yourself at the wheel. "Just steer 185," the captain will tell you as he goes off to take care of some other job. The compass is labeled 180 and 210, so figuring out which little mark is 185 isn't hard, but every time that mark moves away from the pointer you invariably turn the wheel the wrong way and go farther off course. Don't worry, this is not some nautical form of dyslexia. The problem is that your brain thinks the compass card (with the numbers) is rotating. It isn't. It *always* points north. You and the boat are doing the rotating. The card is sitting still, so what you need to know is which way the needle moved, which is also the way the boat moved. If, for example, the compass reads 175 instead of 185, the needle—and the boat—have moved left. Turn to the right to correct.

Don't go blind trying to keep the needle right on 185. Relax. Look away. Watch what is in front of you. Every few seconds just glance at the compass. If you're off course, don't throw the wheel over to get back. Just turn it a little bit. The next time you look, you should be closer to your course; if not, move the wheel a little farther. You will gently curve back and forth across your course. That's fine. The more you sail the less you'll look at the compass and, ironically, the straighter you'll steer.

Sitting at the wheel and maintaining a compass course, by the way, is not sailing. That's steering. You are sailing when you are the one setting the sails.

Where powering is like driving, sailing is more akin to flying. The same principle that lifts a 747 off the ground also "lifts" a sailboat into the wind. You need not understand this principle to fly or to sail, but if you do, it demystifies sailing.

Let's say you and a friend are on one side of a circular running track. Your friend follows the curved track around while you walk straight across the grass infield, and you both get to the opposite side at the same time. Which of you was going faster? It is the same with an airplane wing. The air flowing over the curved top surface of the wing has to go faster to rejoin the air making the shorter straight-line trip underneath. This increase in speed results in a corresponding decrease in pressure, so that now you have more air pressure pushing up on the wing than down on it. This force is appropriately called *lift,* and the faster the air passes over the wing, the more lift the wing develops. At about 180 knots, the 213-foot-long wings of a 747 develop enough vertical lift to pick the 400-ton plane off the ground. We call it flying.

In a sailboat the wing, or *airfoil,* sits vertically, so the "lift" is horizontal—more like pull. We don't need much lift to pull a slippery sailboat through the water, and we can get enough from just the wind blowing over the sail. The only trick is to orient the sail to get the most lift.

Sailboats can't sail directly into the wind. The wind just passes at the same speed on either side of the fluttering sail. Most boats must point at least 45° away from the wind before the sail "fills" and takes on the winglike shape that generates lift and pulls the boat forward. This 45° relationship between sail and wind is all you need to know to make your boat sail.

No matter what direction you want the boat to travel, the first step is to determine where the wind is coming from by looking at the wind vane on the top of the mast, watching ribbon or yarn telltales tied to the rigging, or simply by turning your head until the wind feels the same on both cheeks. Let the sail line up with the wind and it flutters like a flag, but pull in the back part of the

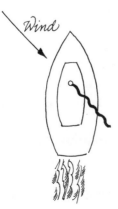
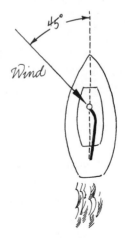

sail to make it break the wind flow by about 45° and it takes on the needed wing shape. That's it. Make the sail break the flow of wind at about 45° and the boat will go in the direction the bow points.

In actual practice you can find the best angle by letting the sail out until it starts to flutter, then tightening it until the fluttering just stops. Here the sail will be the most efficient. Keep in mind that no matter what direction you want the boat to travel, the relationship between the sail and the apparent wind should still be about 45°—until the wind gets far behind you. Once the wind direction gets around to about 135° from the bow, you won't be able to let the mainsail out any farther because of the rigging, but by the time the wind is that far aft, the boat is being pushed more than pulled anyway. When the wind is behind, set the sail perpendicular to the flow of the wind.

Sailing is easy; sailing well takes practice. There are alternate sail combinations, other strings to pull to alter the shape of the sail, steering tricks to keep the boat moving, ballast issues, and the effects of wave action. It is all the variables, the fact that no two days of sailing are alike, that can keep sailing interesting for a lifetime.

Approaching a Dock

Eventually every cruising boat has to go to a dock—to take on fuel or water, or to clear customs. The driver may have wind, current, and tight quarters to contend with, while the crew is supposed to get a dockline attached and keep the boat from hitting the dock. It can be traumatic for both, and often is.

The first step is preparation. Stop the boat away from the dock to assess the conditions, then develop an approach strategy, preferably into the wind and the current so these two forces will tend to carry the boat away from the dock in the event of a missed approach.

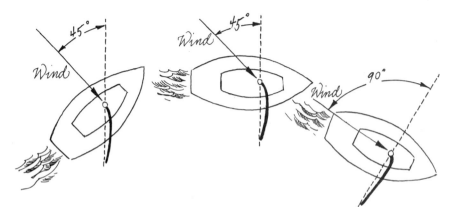

Get docklines ready. Cleat the ends of the lines, then lead them through the chocks and back over the lifelines. Coil them loosely on deck.

Get fenders ready. If you are going against a seawall, you can hang the fenders over the side, but if you are going to a dock with pilings, the fenders offer little protection and can hang up and cause damage. You will be better off with the fenders just ready to be positioned where they are needed. This is why a sturdy rubrail is so valuable on a cruising boat.

Rule #1. In a contest between a 100-something-pound sailor and a 5- or 10-ton boat, *the boat always wins.* Never try to stop a moving boat by sticking out an arm or a leg. Your effort won't make any appreciable difference and you are likely to be injured. If you can't get a fender in place, let the boat hit. Boat repairs are the cheaper and less painful alternative.

The person at the helm should approach the dock dead slow, maintaining only enough speed to retain control. Circumstances occasionally require a more bold approach, but slow is the norm. With a slow approach the helmsman can stop the boat quickly with a burst of reverse power.

When there is no help on the dock, you can sometimes just step from the stopped boat onto the dock and take the appropriate dockline with you. Remember that if you cleat the bow line while the boat is still moving forward, it will pull the bow into the dock. The best line to get ashore first is almost always one attached to the middle of the boat. This is called a *springline,* and if the boat is moving forward, or even backward, this center springline

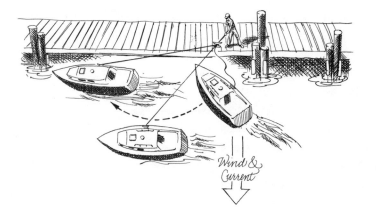

Wind & Current

pulls the boat in parallel to the dock. Unfortunately few boats have midship cleats to accommodate this line.

When the dock is too high to step onto, you will be trying to reach around a piling or jump-rope a loop over it. Regardless of how you get a line ashore, the essential thing is to not stand there holding one end of it. Get it fastened to the cleat or piling, then you can move quickly to help get a second line ashore. Once two lines are attached, most other problems can be sorted out later, including positioning fenders between the pilings and the hull.

Knots

Going to the dock points out the need to attach a line in such a way that it doesn't come loose, a skill that is particularly important aboard a sailboat. But despite all the knot books around, you really only need to know how to cleat a line and tie three knots.

One of these is the *square knot,* and you first learned to tie this one in kindergarten. It is the same knot you use on shoelaces and maybe on scarves. The square knot is used aboard a sailboat mostly to tie things down—the furled sail, for example—and consequently it is also called a *reef knot.* It is made by tying an overhand knot and then a second one in reverse. For shoelaces you make a bow knot by using loops of line rather than the ends for the second overhand knot. You can do it the same way on the boat if you want to be able to release the knot easily.

The only thing you have to watch out for when tying a square knot is that you reverse the second overhand. In other words, if the right line starts under the left one for the first overhand knot, the left one must start underneath for the second knot. If you make both knots the same, you end up with a granny knot. That's exactly what happened the last time you had a hard time getting shoelaces untied.

The easiest knot to use to tie a dockline to a piling is *two half hitches.* After you lead the line around the piling once or twice, pass it on beneath itself, then bring the end back over and drop it between the line and the piling. This is a half hitch. Make a second half hitch outside the first one. Pull both hitches tight, and the line will be securely attached. When the dockline is  too long, you can still tie this knot using a bight of the line instead of the end.

The most useful knot aboard a sailboat is the *bowline.* This is the usual knot for tying sheets to sails, but it can also be used to attach an anchor, to tie two lines together, and to put a loop—fixed or a sliding—in the end of a line to drop over a cleat or piling. The easiest way to learn it? The rabbit comes out of the hole, runs around the tree, and dives back into the hole. Don't move your lips and no one will know.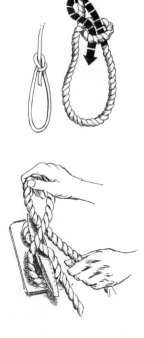

All that is left is putting a line on a cleat. The proper way is with *two turns and a single hitch.* Pass the line under both horns, then diagonally across the top of the cleat twice. Finish with a single hitch, which you form by twisting the last loop ½ turn before you slide it over the cleat horn and pull the end tight. Additional hitches are unnecessary and a nuisance when it is time to release the line. The only trick to cleating a line is to make the half-twist in the right direction. You should recognize immediately when you do it wrong because the last turn doesn't cross the cleat.

Here's a bonus. An overhand knot—half of a square knot—tied in the end of a line can serve as a stopper knot to keep sheets and halyards from getting away, but the *figure eight knot* is much easier to untie later. Tie it just like it sounds.

Anchoring

Because anchors and chain are heavy, the strongest person aboard should normally be the one handling the anchors, but even if you are normally at the helm, knowing how to anchor the boat is an important emergency skill. Likewise you should be able to get the anchor(s) up.

Conveniently lowering and raising the anchor requires a robust anchor roller at the bow. If your boat doesn't have a bow roller, be sure one is fitted before you go cruising. A pair of leather work gloves makes anchor handling less damaging to your hands. We install snaps in a pair of gloves and on the deck at the bow so the gloves are always handy.

Few cruising boats carry a single anchor line—called a *rode*—long enough to effectively anchor in water deeper than about 100 feet, so check the depth in an emergency before you think about anchoring as an option.

The first step in anchoring is to decide where the anchor should be placed. Keep in mind that the boat will end up several boat lengths from the anchor, so don't drop it too close to shallows, shore, or other boats. Observe which way other boats are facing; that is the way you will also settle, with the anchor ahead. In clear water try to pick a sandy patch for the anchor.

Stop the boat. Never just drop the anchor and chain in a lump; the chain will become entangled in the anchor and prevent it from gripping the bottom. If you have an all-chain rode on a windlass, make sure the chain streams out behind the anchor by letting the boat start drifting backward on the wind or current before you release the brake. If you are lowering the anchor by hand, lower it until you feel it hit the bottom. Wait for the boat to start drifting back, then feed out anchor line at the speed of the drift so that it stretches out but you aren't dragging the anchor. Run the line under the horn of a bow cleat before it goes to the roller so you can stop it with the friction against the cleat.

Anchor rodes should be marked every 10, 20, or 50 feet. When you've let out rode equivalent to about five times the depth of the water, cleat the line or tighten the windlass brake. The boat should quit drifting sideways and point toward the anchor—which it will do 99 times out of 100. If it doesn't, the anchor isn't holding. Try letting out two more depth-lengths of rode. If the anchor still drags, pick it up and try again in a different spot.

Always remember that the more line you let out, the more horizontal the pull on the anchor will be, and the better the anchor will hold.

Lifting the anchor is more difficult than lowering it, especially when it is well dug in. The trick is to shorten the anchor rode until it is straight down. In light air you can easily pull the boat to the anchor hand-over-hand, but when the wind is blowing, you will need help. If the boat has an anchor

windlass, push the button or install the handle and crank in the rode. You can accomplish the same thing with a rope rode by taking it to a winch on the mast or in the cockpit, but using the engine to move the boat forward will be easier.

Getting the anchor up alone requires a bit of juggling. Your main concern is not to run over the anchor line so it won't become entangled in the prop. Pick up the rode a little at a time. Start the engine. Put it in gear and steer toward the anchor. As soon as the boat starts to move forward, take it out of gear. You don't want a propeller spinning while you have slack in the anchor rode. Go quickly to the bow and pull in the slack your forward motion has created and cleat the shortened rode. Go back to the helm and jog the boat forward again. Repeat this process until the anchor line is straight down.

There is no reason to pull and tug and grunt trying to break an anchor out of the bottom. Just get the line straight up and down. The wave action will put the inertia of your multi-ton boat to work lifting the anchor for you. It will soon be free, and you will have reserved your energy for hauling it aboard. If there isn't any wave action, try rocking the boat from the stern.

Sea Legs

Motion sickness is a common malady in the first days of a cruise, but strike this from your dread list because there is a better than even chance you won't be affected. If you do feel queasy, there are some effective remedies, which you will find later in this book. Even if you don't do anything but lie down, you'll be over it in a day or so, and that is likely to be it for the remainder of the cruise.

Expect a few bruises in those early days. It takes some time to adapt to walking on a surface that sometimes lurches away from your foot and other times rushes up to meet it. Move around the boat with great deliberation until you get your "sea legs."

You will also be tired in the first days, partly because of nerves, but mostly because your body will be constantly compensating for the motion of the boat. Learn early to relax and let your body move with the boat rather than fighting the motion. This conserves a lot of energy, but don't be surprised if it also makes you sleepy. If you don't have any appointments, hey, give into it. You'll get on cruising time sooner if you do.

A sailboat underway almost always puts life at a slant. Whenever you're

moving around on a boat underway, always have a grip on something. This requires plenty of well-placed handholds, and if you can't go from one end of the boat to the other—both above and below deck—without releasing your grip, the boat needs additional handholds. Learn how to brace yourself first when you need both hands.

Where Are You?

It is sheer folly not to know where you are. In these days of GPS, knowing your position on the globe is often as easy as reading the display. Learn to turn on the GPS and which buttons to push to display your current position. Learn how to determine the same information from a position dot on the chart. This is your address, and it changes by miles every hour. Imagine calling 911 from a cellular phone and when the operator asks where you are, you say New York. Or you say I'm on the road, but I was a few miles from Ithaca this morning. How likely is help to find you? The same thing applies if you don't know where you are when you call for help from your boat.

Make it a habit to mentally note your position three or four times a day. (This is also a good log entry.) In an emergency you may be able to read your immediate position from the GPS, but suppose the emergency disables the GPS, or there just isn't time to fire it up. If you know where you were four hours earlier, and you know what direction and how fast you've been sailing, saying you are approximately 22 miles north-northwest of latitude 24 degrees 33 minutes north and longitude 74 degrees 56 minutes west will pin down your position fairly closely. It's a lot better than saying you're somewhere east of the Bahamas.

Speaking Sailor

If you bought a computer recently, you had to add modem and megabyte and CD-ROM to your vocabulary. And you had to learn new meanings for old words like mouse and window and icon. Sailing also has a rich and colorful language, which you will pick up as you cruise, but there are a handful of words you should know when you start out.

Bow—The front of the boat.

Stern—The back of the boat

Starboard—Starboard means right. It is where the rudder—the steer board—used to be on ancient Dutch vessels, which by convention was on the right side of the boat.

Port—Port means left. To protect the rudder on the right, the Dutch merchantmen put the left side of the boat against the dock, hence it was the port side. To keep this straight until it becomes automatic, just remember that the short words—port and left—mean the same. Port wine, by the way, is red—a good way to remember the color of the port running light.

Halyard—The line used to hoist a sail. (They used to haul *yards,* the horizontal spars supporting square sails.) All the lines running up the mast are halyards. They are specifically identified by what sail they hoist: main halyard, jib halyard, etc.

Sheet—The line that adjusts the angle the sail makes with the wind. *Sheet* is also used as a verb meaning adjust the angle of the sail— "sheet the main in" or even "sheet it out." Sheets are either attached directly to the sail or to the boom.

Boom—The horizontal spar at the bottom of a triangular sail. Also the sound said spar makes when your head gets in the way.

Luff—The leading edge of a triangular sail. Also, the trembling of the forward part of a sail. Adjust the mainsail by letting the boom out until the sail starts to luff, then sheet it in to "put it to sleep."

Fall off—To turn the bow of the boat farther from the wind. When the sails start to luff, you fall off to quiet them.

Come up—The opposite of fall off. To bring the bow of the boat closer to the wind.

Reef—To reduce the size of a sail. In stronger winds less sail area is needed to power the boat, so you reef the sail to make it smaller.

Furl—To roll or fold a sail to secure it when it isn't in use.

Lee—The downwind side. Opposite windward. You anchor in the lee of an island.

Knowing the term that means precisely what you are trying to say always improves communication, no matter what the language. These few sailing terms will get you to your first anchorage.

There is something special about working in concert to handle a boat smartly. For a couple it can be the perfect metaphor for their lives together. At critical moments each member of the crew knows intuitively what to do to compliment the actions of the other, and the boat responds well to such sure hands.

8

8

Safety

DESPITE ALL EVIDENCE TO THE CONTRARY, IT IS HARD NOT TO THINK OF venturing out onto the ocean as more dangerous than driving across Kansas. At least on land, help is never far, and if you survive the accident, you can walk away.

In fact, given a sound boat, little about cruising is inherently dangerous. The way most of us do it, it is a relatively sedate activity. We spend most of our time at anchor, within swimming distance of shore, and when it is time to move on to the next tranquil harbor, we wait out boisterous weather.

As uneventful as that sounds, and usually is, it would be foolhardy to assume that cruising is without risk. There is always ample water around to drown in. The boom can be like a length of pipe in the hands of a violent 300-pound mugger. And if enough water gets inside the boat, it will certainly sink.

Fortunately avoiding the worst consequences of such risks requires little more than being vigilant and taking some precautions.

Staying Aboard

The most serious risk on a boat is falling overboard. The usual response to this threat is the recommendation to wear a life jacket. Boating regulations require one for every person aboard, but few cruising sailors would consider a life jacket everyday apparel. This isn't irresponsibility. Quite to the contrary, cruising sailors recognize that a much better alternative to floating when you fall overboard is not falling overboard at all. A strong safety harness keeps you on board in all conditions, and every cruiser should have one.

Try on several harnesses before you buy one. The one you select should be easy to get into; vest-type harnesses can be easier to put on in a hurry. A harness must be comfortable enough to wear all the time. It has to have enough adjustment to fit your bare body and also go over your foul-weather gear. Some combine with an inflatable life jacket to give you both levels of protection. Some foul-weather jackets have a harness built in.

The tether from your harness should be strong and have two clips so you can attach yourself to a new anchor point before releasing the old one. Equipping your boat with *jacklines*—strongly attached cables or webbing stretched along side decks—lets you go forward without reclipping.

When the boat is underway, especially offshore, it is good seamanship to wear a harness any time you are on deck alone, any time you leave the cockpit, any time sea conditions make footing treacherous, and always at night. Clip on all the time and you'll have all conditions covered—and you almost totally eliminate the risk of falling overboard.

Learn how to make a quick return by tossing a floating cushion overboard and going back for it. The fastest way back is usually the *quick-stop procedure.* If the GPS is on, punch the MOB button to save the position. (If

this were a real emergency, this would also be the time to toss the life ring and/or some cockpit cushions into the water.) Now immediately turn into the wind and tack the boat, even if the incident occurs while you are sailing downwind. Let the headsail backwind. Continue turning to get the wind abeam and sail this beam reach two or three boat lengths, then turn the boat downwind. Now is the time to quickly furl or drop the headsail. Blow downwind until the overboard cushion is slightly behind abeam, then jibe the boat (keep your head down) and sail back to the cushion. If everyone aboard is clipped on, you'll never need this procedure to recover a person, but it is equally effective for recovering a favorite hat that suddenly takes flight.

Injury

Personal injury is next on the risk list. A sailboat is a big machine with lots of parts, some under powerful loads, and both the boat and its parts are given to sudden and unexpected motions. If you position yourself in front of any part that might move, it is like that hand-slapping game you play with kids, except it is a 10-ton boat doing the slapping.

Keep your head below the boom. Don't sit where the mainsheet runs. Keep your fingers clear of blocks and anchor lines. Wear shoes on deck. Make sure nonskid surfaces really are. Don't leave knives and heavy objects lying around below. Replace any cabinet latch you have to stick your finger into. Wear your (bib-front) foul-weather pants or a rubber apron when cooking underway.

Most injuries are preventable with just reasonable caution. In more than 20 years of sailing and cruising, our worst injury came from stepping on a piece of glass on the beach.

Fire

Fire is next. Safe wiring and common cautions with fuels minimize this risk, but you should know where the fire extinguishers are and how to use them.

Flooding

Flooding is every sailor's nightmare. The most common source of flooding at anchor is water siphoning in through the toilet. Underway it is offset sinks that dip below the waterline when the boat heels. Check these first if you see water running across the cabin sole.

Another common source of flooding, believe it or not, is the bilge pump siphoning water *into* the boat because heeling has put the discharge fitting under water. The pump cycles until it depletes the battery, then the water rises. Installing a buzzer or light that tells you when the bilge pump is running is a worthwhile safety precaution.

Through-hull fittings are the next most likely sources of sudden flooding, often from something as simple as a disconnected hose. Know where every through-hull fitting is and be sure you can shut off every seacock in the boat. Seacocks also fail, so you should know where the wooden plugs are to jam into the hole. One ought to be tied to each seacock.

A collision with a submerged object can put a hole in the hull below the waterline that lets water in. If you can find it, you can stem the flow by pressing cushions or bedding or whatever you have into the hole. Just don't panic. Think about how long it takes a bathtub to fill. It takes a lot of water to sink a boat.

A boat can founder in bad weather, but it requires stupidity—leaving hatches open—or a structural failure such as a hatch smashed in or a cockpit locker lid ripped off. You are very unlikely to encounter boat-sinking weather. Should it happen, focus your first efforts on closing the hole, then worry about the water that is already aboard.

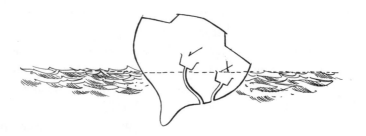

Sinking

If it becomes clear that you are in peril of sinking, the first thing to do is get out of your harness and put on warmer clothes and your life jacket. Then get on the radio and send out a Mayday, giving your position.

If you have a life raft aboard, now is the time to inflate it. Make sure you know how. And be sure the inflating raft is securely attached to the boat. More than one sailor has yanked the cord to inflate a life raft, only to watch it blow away. Pretty disheartening.

Some nautical pundit said "Don't abandon the ship until you have to step up to the life raft." Good advice. Stay with the big boat as long as it floats. It has lockers full of food and tanks full of fresh water, and it is much easier than a raft for rescuers to spot. The number of times abandoned boats are found months later still afloat is testimony that boats are more reluctant to sink than you might imagine. Get food, water, and other supplies into the raft, and go there yourself if you like, but stay tethered to the boat. Don't abandon it until it sinks.

Calling for Help

The decision to call for help can be a hard one, especially offshore. Once you issue such a call, you can't change your mind when help arrives. If, for example, a ship alters course to pick you up, you are obligated to let the crew rescue you, which almost certainly means abandoning your boat. That is a bad time to realize your trouble isn't as serious as you first thought. Don't risk your life to save your boat—boats can be replaced—but try to be sure the danger is grave and imminent before you mobilize a rescue.

There is a "procedure" for sending out a distress call, but all you really need to know is to turn your VHF to channel 16 or your SSB to 2182 (kHz) and say "Mayday, Mayday, Mayday. This is the *Leaky Teaky.* Our position is 24°33′ north and 74°56′ west and we are sinking." Try to speak slowly and clearly, and repeat this information three times. The essential information is Mayday, your position, and your emergency. If you have time, describe your boat and how many are aboard: "We are a 40-foot sailboat, green hull, white decks, with two adults and two children aboard." If someone is injured, mention that.

Don't worry if you don't get a response. That won't necessarily mean no one has heard you. As long as the radio will function, keep periodically sending out a Mayday broadcast, being careful to give your position with every transmission. If time permits, scan through the other channels. Interrupt any radio traffic you hear with your Mayday broadcast. If you don't hear traffic, try transmitting on Coast Guard channels VHF 22a and SSB 2670 kHz.

An SSB radio has greater range, but there are far more VHF radios out there as potential listening stations, and the help you raise on the VHF is likely to be closer. Transmit on both if you have both.

When your emergency is medical in nature, getting a radio response becomes especially important because advice—and sometimes just reassurance—may be all you really need. A radio link with a doctor will be the quickest help you can get, and with a decent first-aid kit aboard you may be able to do exactly what the doctor would do. Far offshore, this is when an SSB or a ham radio returns its investment.

If your emergency isn't immediately life threatening, say Pan-Pan instead of Mayday. This is the urgency call—Pan-Pan, Pan-Pan, Pan-Pan. Make it just like a distress call, except state exactly what assistance you want. For example, maybe you have a controllable leak, and you just want help standing by in case it gets worse. Or the engine has failed and before the batteries get too weak for radio transmission you want to make someone aware of your location, your planned course, and when to consider you overdue. Pan-Pan calls typically result in setting up a radio schedule to keep potential rescuers abreast of your situation. If you fail to keep a radio appointment, the rescue will be mobilized.

Signaling Devices

In an emergency like fire or flooding, radios are often disabled. Boats carry other means of signaling for help. Here is how to use various signaling devices.

EPIRB. An Emergency Position-Indicating Radiobeacon transmits a distress signal to aircraft and satellites. Turn it on and leave it on. It will transmit continuously for at least 48 hours, longer in warm water. In an abandon-ship situation, a working EPIRB is your best assurance of quick rescue.

Pistol-launched aerial flares. Aerial flares look like shotgun shells. Push the release button in the flare pistol and "break" the gun open. Slide the shell into the pistol and snap it shut. Point the pistol nearly straight up, cock the hammer with your thumb, and pull the trigger. Use a flare only when you know someone is around to see it—to attract the attention of a nearby boat or a passing ship, for example.

Meteor flares go a couple of hundred feet up and burn for about 7 seconds. It is a good practice to fire meteor flares in pairs, about 10 seconds apart, because someone observing the first one will often have trouble identifying it or believing it is a distress signal. A second flare confirms for the observer that it was not his or her imagination but a genuine emergency, and it facilitates pinpointing your location.

More expensive parachute flares climb to more than 1,000 feet and burn more than half a minute, generally doing the job adequately with a single shot. Parachute-flare cartridges are about three times as long as a meteor cartridge and protrude beyond the end of the barrel of the launcher. Load and fire them the same way as meteors.

Hand-launched aerial flares. The instructions for hand-launched flares are written on the flare. Some meteor flares screw onto a special "pen" launcher; others have a chain under a screw-cap that you pull to fire the flare.

Hand-launched parachute flares typically have a trigger. Tear off the protective tab or cap, point the flare up, and squeeze the trigger. The whoosh that follows may startle you, but it won't hurt you.

Handheld flares. Handheld flares are intended to help a rescuer pinpoint your location. If you get the attention of a ship with a parachute or meteor flare, lighting a handheld flare will show them where you are. Likewise you can help a search plane find you with a flare, especially at night.

Some handheld flares strike like a match; the tear-off cap houses an abrasive surface you strike against the flare to ignite it. Other brands have some type of firing mechanism that you hit or pull. Lighting instructions are on the flare.

Never hold handheld flares over your head or over a rubber raft. They are like a super Fourth of July sparkler, most raining down a fountain of hot slag. It is imperative that you hold them nearly horizontal, as far away from you as you can, downwind, and over the water, not over the boat or raft.

Signal mirror. In daylight a mirror can be one of the most effective signaling devices, announcing your presence with the intensity of the sun. A signal mirror has a sighting hole in its center, but any mirror can be used to signal. The idea is to reflect the sun into the eyes of a potential rescuer.

To aim a signal mirror, hold two fingers in a V at arm's length, with your target inside the V. Close one eye and, sighting with the other through the aiming hole, adjust the angle of the mirror to throw light on your fingers. Play the light back and forth across your fingers, and it will also play across the target inside the V. If your mirror doesn't have a sighting hole, hold it against your cheek just below your eye and aim it the same way.

Safety in Your Pockets

Attach a loud whistle to your safety harness. With it you can immediately summon off-watch help in a sudden emergency. Life jackets and other flotation devices should also be equipped with a whistle. It is much more effective than a shout in helping locate a person in the water.

A personal strobe light is another valuable safety item. Gear failure or human error can defeat even a harness, and a strobe makes you infinitely easier to locate at night.

With all the potentially entangling lines aboard a boat, a knife can literally be a lifesaver. Get in the habit of carrying one. It doesn't have to be big or heavy, and you can clip it to your harness or stuff it in your pocket. Keep it sharpened.

Do You Need a Life Raft?

You are booking a vacation flight and Legacy Air is $800 while upstart Cheapo Jet will fly you to the same destination for $299. What do you do? It probably depends on how risky you think a Cheapo Jet flight is.

The liferaft decision is similar. What is the risk on your planned cruise that you are going to have to abandon your boat at sea? If your cruise is along the coast, a dinghy that you can motor or row to shore may well be adequate or even preferable. But if your track takes you well offshore, a life raft becomes the only viable option for coping with the unthinkable.

Ocean racers are required to carry life rafts, but cruisers make ocean passages every day without a life raft. For most it is a purely financial decision, not unlike cruising without insurance. But, of course, the absence of a raft is a gamble not with money but with lives.

Given a well-found boat, would I make an occasional overnight passage in good weather without a life raft aboard? Sure. Beyond that, the variables multiply, and so do the risks. The essential truth is that if life rafts were free, no one would sail without one aboard.

The survival supplies packed in virtually every brand of life raft are so meager as to be ludicrous. If you have a life raft aboard, you should also have a "going-away bag" near the companionway that contains at least a watermaker or water, food, the EPIRB, a handheld VHF, flares, a signal mirror, a flashlight, warm clothing including watch caps, space blankets, wet or dry suits, a first-aid kit that includes sunblock and vitamins, fishing gear, a knife and a cutting board, plastic bags, sponges, raft patches, a lashing cord, a chart, a compass, and a survival manual.

Oh yeah, also be sure your grab bag includes a waterproof camera and writing materials. If your boat actually does sink at sea, your misfortune will be so notable that a book deal is almost a certainty.

The sense of insignificance you feel facing a vast and powerful ocean becomes over time less frightening and more humbling. And there is something wonderfully freeing about knowing you aren't in control. Not being in control, however, is not the same thing as not being prepared. Be sure essential safety equipment is aboard, and be sure you know how to use it.

9

Staying in Touch

"WHAT IF SOMETHING HAPPENS TO DAD?"

It is a question that strikes a nerve with most cruisers, reluctant or otherwise.

We are accustomed to being in touch. Family and friends can pick up a telephone and in a matter of seconds have us on the other end of the line, or at least leave a message. The idea of being out of reach for days, perhaps even weeks, can be disturbing. Ironically it isn't good news we're worried about missing.

Communications options for the cruising boat are far more varied than they were even a decade ago, and the technology is evolving at an accelerating pace. As I write this, satellite telephones are already on the market that allow you to phone home from anywhere on the globe, but their current cost excludes most cruisers. Until the price drops—and it will—most of us depend on less expensive systems to link us to shore.

Mail

Before we explore electronic links, perhaps we should deal with correspondence. Can *you* pay your Visa bill and receive your magazine subscriptions while you're cruising. The answer is no.

The only workable strategy for dealing with mail is to have a permanent address ashore. Most cruisers depend on a family member or a close friend to handle their mail, but there are also a number of professional services in this business. Whoever your shore contact is screens and sorts your mail, usually paying recurring bills based on standing instructions. Unusual correspondence may necessitate trying to reach you or at least adding an item on the agenda for your next call in. Junk mail is discarded, and all that remains is put aside. Some cruisers have all mail packaged and sent to them periodically; others want only letters and such, holding magazines and similar bulky items until they return from the cruise or until someone flies in for a visit.

It is possible to have mail sent ahead of you to General Delivery or to a marina, cruiser-friendly hotel, Barclays Bank, or American Express office. Unfortunately marinas and hotels go out of business or change their mail-receiving policies, and while some post offices still have "Hold for Arrival" packages addressed to Amelia Earhart, others send all mail back if you don't call for it in four or five days—not good when you are days away and waiting on weather. Barclays and American Express are dependable enough when they actual get the package, but it may get waylaid in customs.

Olga and I have almost always found it less frustrating to wait until we know exactly what the situation is where we are, then call home and have a package mailed or, even better, couriered to us. A driver's license is adequate identification to pick up mail in the United States, but you will generally be asked to show your passport in foreign countries. Have your mail forwarder write your name *in block letters* exactly as it appears on your passport.

Early on in a cruise, loose ends ashore can generate an annoying amount of seemingly urgent correspondence, but the longer you cruise, the fewer pieces of mail you will receive that your shore contact can't handle without you. Mail is almost always a bigger worry before you leave than after you've been cruising for a few months.

VHF Radio

The lowly VHF radio remains the most versatile communication device for a boat. It is the *only* communication device most pleasure boats carry, and it is required by law before you can put any other marine radio aboard. This universality makes VHF arguably the most valuable piece of safety gear aboard, delivering a call for assistance to dozens or hundreds of nearby listening ears.

Cruisers also use the VHF much like a telephone to call other boats and shore stations to relay information, to make appointments, or sometimes just to chat. Before you join in, however, you should recognize the differences between radio and telephone communication.

- ◆ Radio conversations are not private; when you talk on the VHF, everyone within range tuned to that channel is listening.
- ◆ Regulations require radio conversations to be for "operational" purposes, which is interpreted liberally by most pleasureboat operators. Sharing weather information, confirming a rendezvous, even obtaining a recipe are defensible subjects, but social chitchat—say, talk about sports, fashion, or literature—is not. This regulation is widely ignored in remote cruising areas, but if someone calls you down about it, he is right.
- ◆ A radio conversation ties up the channel you are using; no one else within a 30- or 40-mile radius can use it until you sign off. This is significant because only five channels are legitimately available for pleasureboat-to-pleasureboat communication. Think of this situation as an airport terminal with a single bank of five pay phones. If callers are lined up three-deep while some blockhead drones on and on about the size of the mosquitoes in Maine, you can be sure he won't be the only unhappy camper. In high-traffic areas, keep calls short.

The VHF radio is also capable of placing telephone calls to and receiving them from anywhere in the world as long as your cruise never takes you more than about 50 miles from the coast. It is simply a matter of calling the nearest marine operator and telling him or her what number you wish to reach. Someone trying to reach you dials the marine operator, and notification that you have incoming "traffic" is announced on channel 16. Cost for this service is a modest subscription fee (currently about $35 a *year*), and a flat-rate connect charge of about $1.50 per minute to any U.S. number.

If you want to use your VHF to make telephone calls, subscribe to the service before you leave. Leave anyone who might need to reach you a rough itinerary, because the service provider will need to know which marine operator should be announcing your traffic. Since to receive an incoming call you have to be monitoring channel 16 when your traffic is announced, this service is more reliable for calls placed from the boat, so it may be easier to stay in touch with periodic calls you initiate. By the way, marine operators don't monitor channel 16, so even though they call you on this channel, you must respond on the operator's working channel.

Like all VHF transmissions, VHF telephone conversations are public to anyone who wants to listen in on the marine operator channel, but regulations regarding the nature of your conversation do not apply.

A low-cost, low-tech way of staying reachable during your cruise is to maintain a scheduled radio watch on VHF. If, for example, you have your VHF radio on and tuned to channel 16 every morning between 8 and 9 A.M. EST, and those ashore who might need to reach you know that, it will be much easier to get a call to you through the marine operator. Further, the Coast Guard, in a genuine emergency, can raise you on the radio during your scheduled watch and relay a message. It might even be possible to orchestrate a boat-to-boat relay to reach you far beyond the range of the Coast Guard transmission.

Using a VHF radio is as easy as announcing yourself on an apartment intercom. Turn the power on, set the channel to 16, and listen for a few seconds. If 16 isn't in use, key the microphone—meaning squeeze the button on its side—and say "*Yellowbird, Yellowbird. Seabreeze,* over." Release the mike button. You can say "This is *Seabreeze,*" but keeping calls as cryptic as possible is desirable. Since VHF licensing was eliminated (except for vessels traveling into foreign waters), you no longer need to announce your radio call sign.

Yellowbird will respond "*Seabreeze,* (this is) *Yellowbird.*"

If *Yellowbird* doesn't respond, wait 2 minutes and try again. You are permitted three tries 2 minutes apart, but common sense should tell you that if *Yellowbird* has failed to respond twice, the third transmission is just airwave pollution. Wait at least 15 minutes before you make another attempt. Few things will give your cruising neighbors a worse opinion of you than listening to you call over and over and over. *They're not there, already; give it a rest.*

When *Yellowbird* does respond, key your mike and say "Six eight?" Channel 16 is reserved exclusively for calling and distress. Once contact is established, you must switch to a working channel. The five channels designated for noncommercial ship-to-ship communications are 68, 69, 71, 72, and 78. Channel 9 used to be in this group but has been redesignated as an alternate calling (but not distress) channel.

Yellowbird confirms by saying "Six eight."

By either rotating a knob or pushing a button, you select channel 68 on your radio, key the mike, and say *"Yellowbird. Seabreeze."*

When *Yellowbird* responds, you have your conversation, ending each transmission with "over" so *Yellowbird* will know when you are finished and it is time to respond. When your conversation is complete, your last transmission should be *"Seabreeze,* out."

Yellowbird will likewise say *"Yellowbird,* out." "Out" lets anyone waiting to use the channel know you are through with it.

Sometimes when you switch to a working channel, you find it occupied. In that case, check the other four to find an empty one, then go back to 16 and say, *"Yellowbird. Seabreeze.* Seven one." If you and *Yellowbird* speak regularly, saying just "seven one" may be adequate.

Either way, *Yellowbird* will respond "seven one." You both switch to channel 71 and have your conversation.

All fixed-mount VHF radios can transmit at either 25 watts or 1 watt. If your radio contact is nearby, set the power setting to low to reduce the distance the signal carries beyond your target. Also watch your language; not only is profanity over the air against the law, it will be particularly offensive to cruisers with children aboard.

High-Seas Radio

Marine SSB (single-sideband) radio has a much longer range than VHF, exceeding 10,000 miles in the right conditions. Unfortunately this extra range comes dear: good SSB installations have for several years hovered around $2,000, making them about 10 times as expensive as VHF. On the other hand, SSB will summon help when no VHF station is within range.

SSB isn't just a souped-up VHF. All-frequency capability means an SSB radio can receive worldwide international broadcast stations, providing you with the latest news. Perhaps more important, it fetches all the latest weather wisdom out of the ether, and when supplemented with a weatherfax or a laptop PC, allows you to see up-to-the-minute weather charts for your area. It links you to the many marine nets—daily chat sessions among sailors that can yield valuable information about places you are headed. The SSB radio can deliver music, talk, and other entertainment to the most remote locations.

These features aside, the overriding reason most cruisers put SSB aboard is to have offshore or "down-island" ship-to-shore capabilities. Simply put, a marine SSB radio will let you phone home from anywhere in the world and, with some limitations, let home phone you.

As with VHF, you should register with one or more high-seas telephone service providers before you leave. The cost to make a high-seas call is currently about $5 per minute with a three-minute minimum.

Operation of a marine SSB radio is somewhat more complicated than VHF because you have so many more frequency choices, and also because transmission is affected by the time of day—meaning that some "bands" have long ranges in the daylight hours and others "reach out" only at night. While 2182 kHz is the international distress frequency, SSB radios have no "call frequency." Individual connections, unless they happen by chance, require a prearranged schedule. This is the primary reason for radio nets, to provide a known time and frequency for meeting—not unlike going to a bar or dropping in to an Internet chat room. If your party is on the net, you can move to an alternate frequency, or schedule a future contact.

For ship-to-shore communication, you dial up the appropriate frequency (each high-seas service operates on 15 or 20 frequencies) and call the station using both their call sign and yours—"WOM, WOM, WOM, this is *Seabreeze*, WXY4567." SSB radios require a station license, and you are required to give your call sign both when you sign on and when you sign off. Calling the high-seas operator is the one time when repeating your call over and over is appropriate. The automated equipment may not recognize you unless your call lasts for 30 seconds or more, so just keep repeating the call until you get an answer. Giving your approximate location—"I am near 24 degrees north, 75 degrees west"—will help telephone-station technicians select the best antenna for your transmission. When the operator responds, follow his or her instructions.

High-seas operators announce waiting traffic and give ocean weather conditions every four hours, transmitting simultaneously on all their frequencies. Switching bands during this broadcast is a foolproof way of determining the best frequency to use for your call—the one where their transmission is the clearest.

Once you make contact, carrying on a conversation over the SSB is very similar to using the VHF. Key the mike to talk, release it to listen, and end every transmission with "over." The best way to get comfortable with SSB protocol is just to listen for a few days to different frequencies on various bands. Nets in particular follow certain conventions to prevent them from becoming chaotic.

The Ham Alternative

Obtain the necessary license and you can stay in touch by operating a mobile amateur radio station. A licensed amateur-radio operator is called a *ham*.

Ham radio and marine SSB are very similar in transmission range and other features. In fact, although it is illegal to do so, a simple modification to a ham transceiver will allow it to also broadcast on all the marine SSB frequencies. A few years ago marine SSB radios were priced as high as $5,000, whereas ham sets that would do almost the same thing were selling for about $700. This was the genesis for ham radio's popularity aboard cruising boats. Today marine SSB radios are only about twice the price of similar ham sets, but the ham network has become firmly established among cruisers.

Let me make it clear that ham radio and marine SSB are not the same thing. No one is monitoring any ham frequency for distress calls, so it is not a reliable link for a sudden emergency. You cannot contact the high-seas operator on the ham bands. Amateur radio rules prohibit doing *any* business on the air, so even if another ham patches through a telephone call for you, it can't be to order parts or supplies.

You simply "buy" a station license to operate a marine SSB radio, but you need a test-obtained *operator's* license to transmit on any amateur band. The advanced (General class) license needed to transmit on the bands that offer worldwide range requires you to pass a series of tests on radio theory and to demonstrate your ability to receive Morse code at 13 words per minute. Not that getting your ham license is all that difficult, but it does generally require two to three months of study and code practice.

A ham set is also much more complicated to use than marine SSB. With the SSB set, you simply dial in the frequency, key the mike, and you are on the air. A typical ham set will have more than 20 controls you have to set, switch, or twiddle to get the radio adjusted just right for your transmission.

Ham radio, however, has one big advantage: it is not marine radio. It is illegal to operate marine radios—both VHF and SSB—from shore. This technically includes calling the boat from the dock with a handheld VHF. Only marine-related businesses like marinas and telephone operators are issued shore permits. But since you can operate a ham radio anywhere, there is no reason that ol' Dad can't go to radio classes with you and get his own ham license. Put a transceiver in the den and you can call home every day if you like.

Even if Dad doesn't become a ham, it won't be hard to find a local ham that will be happy to patch through a periodic telephone call. Just as important, the local ham can get a message to you in an emergency at home.

If you are willing to do the work to get your license, ham radio is the least expensive way of staying in touch offshore or in remote cruising grounds. A mobile ham station, including an automatic antenna tuner, runs about $1,300 today, and per-minute costs are nonexistent—prohibited, in fact. A ham set can also keep you in contact with other cruisers you meet. And if you become fascinated by the possibilities, as many do, a ham station can introduce you to other hams all over the world.

Beepers

Two-way pagers are now available that let you respond to messages you receive. This has the potential to be just what a cruiser needs to stay in touch. You are offshore when the beeper goes off, and the message says, "Mom broke hip." There is nothing you can do until you reach shore, so you key in "St. Thomas 2 days." When you reach St. Thomas, you call home, and fly out if necessary.

Unfortunately this is just fantasy. While some pager services now offer what their advertising calls "national" and "international" coverage, those characterizations are highly optimistic. All this really means is that a caller can page you in a number of domestic and foreign cities. Get more than 20 miles from a major city and your beeper is a worthless lump of colorful plastic.

Even for a cruise along the coast, a so-called national pager service currently costs nearly $50 a month—more than twice the base monthly charge for a cellular phone. Until satellite pagers with per-use cost plans are available, pagers will adequately serve the communication needs of few cruisers.

Cellular Telephones

Except for going ashore and using a pay phone, only placing telephone calls through a VHF marine operator will be less expensive than using a cellular phone (where cell-phone coverage is available).

There are no "equipment costs" to use the marine operator because the VHF radio is aboard for other reasons. A cellular phone is also "free" if you already own one. Even if you don't, many service providers will give you one.

A low annual subscription fee makes VHF cheaper as a standby service. Cellular telephone service typically costs at least $20 a month, but the per minute cost of a cell-phone call, including roaming charges for being outside the local area for your provider, will be less than half the marine operator rate. If you average as much as 20 minutes per month on the phone, the cell-phone becomes the more economical of the two.

For convenience, the cell-phone wins hands down—you just pick up the handset and dial the number you want. More to the point of this chapter, when someone needs to reach you, they simply dial your number. For a small additional fee a message service answers when you can't.

As appealing as this sounds, cell-phone coverage in many prime cruising areas will be limited to population centers, and even where it is available, on-the-water coverage can be spotty at best. If you want to make the most of this communication option, forget portable flip phones and install either a mobile phone or what is called a *transportable*. These units will operate off the ship's battery, virtually eliminating fade-out, but more important, they have a provision for a remote antenna. A special cell-phone antenna mounted as high as possible will extend your offshore range from about 5 miles to perhaps 50 or more. Under ideal conditions, cell-phone calls have reportedly been made more than 300 miles offshore, but don't expect that to occur often.

Satellite Communications

Satellite communications are changing so rapidly that anything I say here will be old news by the time you read it. Still, getting you at least closer to the current situation may be helpful.

Marine satellite telephones have been around since the mid-70s. When you see a big white dome on a ship or a megayacht, it probably contains a gyro-stabilized antenna that lets the rolling and pitching ship maintain its link with the satellite. These first-generation systems cost more than $30,000, and the per-minute cost of placing a call is about $12.

Over the next two decades satellite telephone equipment has gotten progressively smaller and less expensive, and the per minute cost has plunged. Today you can purchase a complete satellite system for your boat for about $5,000. Instead of being more than 4 feet across, the required antenna is about the size of a bicycle helmet, and the per-minute cost is down to a little over $1 for regional coverage, about 3 bucks if you want a worldwide system. With one of these aboard, all anyone needs to do to get in touch with you is dial your number.

But . . . the best is still to come. A number of companies are spending billions of dollars to launch arrays of low-orbit satellites that will reduce the phone-to-satellite distance from about 23,000 miles to maybe 300 miles. That changes everything. The easiest way to picture this is to think of these satellites as very tall cellular-phone "towers." In fact, the idea is that your phone will be a dual-mode cell-phone, trying first to make a land-based link before switching to the satellite. What equipment will you need? Nothing. Just the phone. Pull up the antenna and call Oslo from the South Pacific.

This technology is already available in a very limited way for sending and receiving messages. For about $1,000, you can take aboard a "satellite communicator" that will let you send and receive E-mail messages from anywhere. You can use this equipment only when a satellite is in sight of the transmitter—currently about 10 minutes eight times a day. As additional satellites are launched over the next few years, communication time will expand. Use cost is about a penny per character plus the monthly cost of an E-mail service. Messages are currently limited to 250 characters—about 40 words.

By the time enough satellites are flying to make this satellite "pager"

really convenient, low-orbit satellite phones will be on the market. What will one of these global phones cost? The target price for at least one of the players in the race is $750, and you can expect prices to drop as more users come aboard. The cost per minute is projected to be roughly the same as for cellular service. Partial capability of this system is expected as early as 1998. By the end of the century, you are almost certain to be able to carry a telephone in your pocket that will connect you instantly to any telephone in the world.

Until the future arrives, radio remains the least-cost alternative for staying in touch and more than adequately satisfies the needs of most cruisers. For safety reasons every cruising boat should have a VHF radio aboard. And if your cruise plans will take you well offshore, the additional safety a marine SSB or, to a lesser degree, a ham radio provides, combined with the ability of both to deliver valuable weather and cruising information, makes a long-range radio worthwhile. When you already have a radio aboard with adequate range, staying "reachable" involves little more than setting up a watch schedule. The cost to make an occasional "check-in" call through a marine operator will be nominal.

Without a long-range radio aboard, reaching you in an emergency is more difficult, but as long as those ashore know roughly where you are, contact with local authorities or even a telephone call to a nearby marina can generate a VHF call during your scheduled radio watch. You will also meet cruisers along the way that stay in touch with daily ham transmissions or have a computer or voice satellite link. Most will be happy to tell you how they can be reached in an emergency, and to subsequently orchestrate a relay to get the message to you. Cruisers are a community, and anyone who hears an emergency call for you and knows where you are will respond.

Thankfully, imagined emergencies rarely occur. Thousands of cruisers are routinely out of touch for days or weeks at a time without consequence. It is simply a fact that the unexpected happens, well, unexpectedly. Waiting around for it to happen seems like a bad plan. Go on your cruise and invite family and friends to share it with you. You will all cherish the experience.

10

~

Health and First Aid

LIFE IS FILLED WITH UNCERTAINTY. GOING CRUISING MAY NOT INSULATE YOU from cancer, aneurysm, or turf toe, but it won't increase your exposure either. The risk of drowning may be greater, but you are out of the traffic-statistic pool. And while a few bumps and bruises are likely, colds and allergies are mostly left behind.

The concern of many is less about health and more about health care. We have doctors we trust, around-the-clock emergency rooms, a 911 service that brings medical help in minutes. Even if we haven't needed health care in the last year, we are used to the security of knowing it is at hand.

Cruising doesn't sever your relationship with your doctor. You can call him or her from wherever you are, even from offshore if you have ship-to-shore radio capability. Get a checkup before you go, and tell your doctor your concerns. Almost all will tell you the same thing: "Go live your life." He or she may also be willing to help you customize your first-aid kit for your specific health needs.

If you are relatively healthy when you start out, the likelihood of requiring a doctor, much less emergency care, during a six-month or one-year cruise is small. Should you need medical attention, health care in some form is available in all but the smallest communities. Keep in mind that doctors everywhere, more often than not, simply make you more comfortable; it is your body that does the healing.

Expect Good Health

Here is the operative question: What about cruising is unhealthy?

Is the outdoor life less healthy than being a shut-in? Is the vigorous life less healthy than the sedentary one? Is variety less healthy than routine? Is freedom less healthy than servitude? Is ocean air less healthy than urban smog? Is the beach less healthy than the office? Is sun less healthy than sleet? Is fish less healthy than beef? Is swimming less healthy than running? Is traveling at 7 miles an hour less healthy than at 70?

With the deck stacked so heavily in your favor, illness aboard a cruising boat is unusual. Sure you can catch a cold—or worse—when you're ashore, but the number of close contacts with the walking infirmed will be minuscule compared to the typical office environment.

Injury is a bigger risk, but it can be mostly avoided by being careful. Keep your head lower than the boom. Make sure the sliding hatch is open before starting up the companionway. Use extra caution around the galley stove. Protect your toes on deck by wearing shoes. Hold on. Hold on. Hold on.

Expect to discover healthier eating rhythms. Activity and fresh air give almost everyone a hearty appetite, but you won't be very hungry when it is hot and soporific in the middle of the day. The conventional three-meal schedule is often replaced by a more natural eat-when-you're-hungry routine.

The quality and perhaps the quantity of your sleep will also improve. Underway you may or may not find sleep elusive, but at anchor—where a cruising boat is more than 90 percent of the time—the motion of the boat and the "white sound" of the water flat-lines almost everyone. Afternoon naps are common.

If you are headed toward the tropics, you need three essential sleep aids. The hatch over your bunk *must* be fitted with an effective windscoop that will funnel the slightest zephyr below. One that lets you leave the hatch open through a rain shower will be much appreciated. Second, you need screens for all hatches. Mosquitoes and no-see-ums are much less of a problem at anchor than ashore, but it takes the whine of only a single mosquito to thwart sleep. Finally, you need a cabin fan over your bunk and ample battery power to run it through the night. When the wind dies at night in the tropics, sleep will be

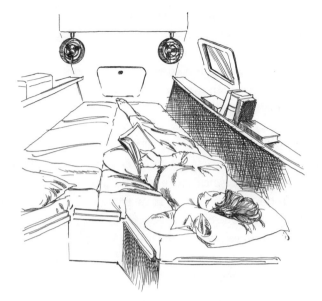

impossible without an effective cabin fan; with a fan you will sleep the sleep of the righteous.

I have mentioned stress before. Cruising does have stressful moments, but it is not the crushing, heart-attack variety we are subjected to ashore. It is more like a stress workout, typically lasting only long enough to get your heart rate up. Climbing a dozen flights of stairs isn't pleasant when you're sucking wind, but doing it regularly improves your condition, and the climb gets easier. Cruising stress is like that.

If you go cruising, you will eat well, sleep well, and discover deep relaxation. You will have more energy, better muscle tone, and your eyesight may even improve. You aren't likely to need a doctor, and probably the only first-aid item you will take out of the box is an occasional Band-Aid.

But You're the Doctor

Cheerleading aside, if you do have illness or injury aboard and you're not the patient, then you're the doctor. It is not a responsibility to take lightly. At the very least, read a current first-aid book before you leave. Better yet, take a first-aid course, and insist that the captain take it with you; he will, after all, be *your* doctor.

First aid has only two requirements:

1. Restore breathing.
2. Stop bleeding.

After you do these two, everything else can be considered *second* aid;

your patient is probably out of imminent danger, and you have time to consult a medical guide or raise a doctor on the radio.

Restoring breathing is most important. Five minutes of not breathing—apnea—will result in brain damage. Many injuries "stun" the brain and cause apnea, so the first thing to check for in any injury is breathing. If you do not observe the injured person's chest rising and falling and you can't feel breathing with your ear near his or her mouth, it is imperative to begin mouth-to-mouth resuscitation immediately. "Breathe" for the victim by blowing into his lungs to expand his chest, then removing your mouth from his to let the breath exhale. Repeat this every 5 seconds until the victim begins to breathe on his own. Continue to help him breathe until his blue-gray lips and earlobes turn pink again.

Stopping bleeding comes second, except in the case of a severed artery "gushing" blood. Most adults can survive losing up to a quart of blood, a lot of blood from a run-of-the-mill laceration. Once you have breathing established, arrest bleeding by putting pressure directly on the wound. Eventually you want to close the wound with a bandage or sutures.

There is much more to effectively administering to every potential injury aboard a cruising boat. You should know how to deal with burns, sprains, broken bones, and cardiac arrest. You should also be able to recognize internal disorders and diagnose various illnesses from their symptoms. Even if you aren't a doctor, you can do all of these with the help of a good medical guide, a number of which are readily available. But as long as you know enough to start the breathing and stop the bleeding, tragedy is unlikely to visit you.

The Medical Library

Olga and I have had three medical texts aboard for two decades, and I am happy to report that we have never had cause to open any of them except out of curiosity and to brush up on our first-aid knowledge before the start of a cruise. Still, I would no more sail without them than start off without an anchor.

Your medical library should include both a first-aid guide for injuries and sudden illness, and a medical guide covering the full spectrum of medical conditions, including their diagnosis, treatment, and prevention. A few books cover both of these in a single volume.

Exactly what book or books should anchor your medical library is a personal choice. A format that is magic for one reader is impenetrable for another. Go to a good bookstore or chandlery and thumb through several medical guides to find one that seems to give you the quickest and/or clearest answers to your medical questions. Finding the various offerings in a bookstore isn't always easy; look in both the "sailing" and the "outdoors" sections as well as "health care."

Here are some suggestions. Start with the Red Cross *Standard First Aid* manual. This is the textbook for the first-aid course you and Skip are going to take before you leave. The American Medical Association *Handbook of First Aid and Emergency Care* is equally informative.

Supplement your basic first-aid book with Dr. Peter Eastman's *Advanced First Aid Afloat,* a well-conceived guide that has been *the* favorite among cruising sailors for 25 years. Or you may prefer Dr. Paul Gill's *Onboard Medical Guide.* An alternative to either of these, or perhaps a complement, is *Where There Is No Doctor,* by David Werner, a medical guide intended for villagers and community workers in remote areas. (The companion *Where There Is No Dentist* might also prove valuable if your cruise lasts more than a few months.)

If you would feel better with a medical guide that covers every imaginable condition, take a look at *The Ship's Medicine Chest and Medical Aid at Sea* put out by the U.S. Department of Health. Intended for merchant ships, this 700-page volume is surely the most comprehensive offshore medical guide available. Some chandleries carry it, but if you can't find it locally, you can order it from the Government Printing Office (Superintendent of Documents, P.O. Box 371954, Pittsburgh, PA 15250-7954).

For diagnostic help, you might add to your library one of the many medical encyclopedias intended for the home. If you have a computer aboard, you can save space with a disk-version medical encyclopedia. A first-aid guide that requires a computer is a bad idea.

The First-Aid Kit

If you are tempted to buy a prepacked first-aid kit, be careful. None of them, no matter how expensive, satisfy more than basic first-aid requirements. That is because the drugs they contain are limited to aspirin, burn cream, and perhaps antiseptic ointment. None contain prescription drugs.

As long as you recognize their limitations, buying a first-aid kit does save you time, but assembling your own will likely save money. More important, when you assemble your own first-aid kit, you know what is in it and presumably why.

Soft packs have become popular for first-aid supplies, but a waterproof box will do a better job of keeping gauze and cotton and the like dry and sterile. Appropriate gasketed tote boxes can be purchased for less than $20.

What goes in the box? No two boats carry identical medical supplies, but here is a list that should help you stock your boat with the basic essentials. Add anything else that raises your confidence for being able to deal with a medical emergency.

BANDAGES

Adaptic nonstick dressings, 3″ × 3″	10
Adhesive strips	1 box assorted sizes
Adhesive strips	1 box 1″-wide
Elastic (Ace) bandage, 3″ or 4″	2
Eye pads	4
Gauze pads, 4″ × 4″	30
Roll bandages (Kerlix), 4″	5 x 5 yards
Steri-Strip skin closures, ¼″ × 3″	2 packs (12)
Steri-Strip skin closures, ½″ × 4″	2 packs (12)
Surgipads, 8″ × 10″	5
Tape, 1″ waterproof	1 roll (12.5 yards)
Triangular bandage	2

INSTRUMENTS

Bulb syringe	1
Cotton swabs	1 package
Dental mirror	1
Oral thermometer	1
Roll-up splint (Sam splint)	2
Safety pins, large	1 package
Scissors for bandages	1 pair
Disposable scalpels	2 (#11 and #15)
Surgical gloves	5 pair
Surgical staples	5
Tongue sticks	12
Tweezers (w/o teeth)	1 pair

NONPRESCRIPTION MEDICINES

Alcohol, isopropyl	1 pint
Ammonia inhalants	6
Antacid, liquid or tablet	1 bottle
Antibiotic ointment (Bacitracin)	1 ounce
Antihistamine (Benadryl—25mg)	1 bottle
Aspirin	100
Betadine	4 ounces
Calamine lotion	8 ounces
Chemical cold pack	4
Desitin ointment	1 tube

Eugenol (oil of cloves liquid)	1 bottle
Eye irrigate	1 ounce
Hydrocortisone ointment 1%	1 tube
Imodium AD	1 package
Monistat	1 package
Motion-sickness tablets	1 card (for guests)
Oral rehydration salts (ORS or Pedialyte)	4 packets
Pepto-Bismol	1 bottle
Petroleum jelly	1 tube
pHisoHex	4 ounces
Sting reliever	1 bottle
Silvadene (burn cream)	400-gram jar
Spenco 2nd Skin (for open blisters)	5 pads
Tincture of benzoin	1 bottle or 12-ounce spray
Tincture of iodine, 2%	1 bottle
Tylenol	1 bottle
Zinc oxide	1 tube
Zinc oxide powder	1 package

Cruises that last for more than a few months and take you away from the United States call for an increased level of self-sufficiency. Prescription drugs are unavailable in many places, and where they are available, they often have unfamiliar names. You should, of course, carry an adequate supply of any prescription drug you require, but it may also be advantageous to take along a few other drugs to deal with medical conditions you *might* encounter.

You can spend quite a few dollars on expensive drugs only to throw them away unopened. *That is exactly what you want to do.* The money you spend on these drugs is not for health care; it is for security.

PRESCRIPTION DRUGS

Adrenaline (Ana-Kit)	bee sting kit
Ampicillin (capsules)	antibiotic
Bactrim DS (tablet)	sulfa drug for urinary infection
Darvocet (tablets)	painkiller
Demerol (capsules)	painkiller
Ephedrine (tablet)	stimulant—effective motion-sickness remedy when combined with promethazine
Lomotil (tablet or liquid)	diarrhea relief—OTC Imodium AD may be just as effective

Promethazine (tablet)	antihistamine
Tetracycline (tablet)	antibiotic
Xylocaine (injection)	local anesthetic—syringe required

This last list is intended merely as a starting point for your own discussion with your physician. I am no doctor, and I am not recommending these particular drugs. They are simply the most common prescription drugs found in cruising-boat medical kits. Few boats carry all of them. Your physician can advise you and may suggest alternatives.

Prescription drugs aboard present some problems. Most have a limited life, and some will need to be refrigerated. If you have a lot of them aboard, and, say, a box of hypodermic syringes, foreign authorities may look askance. And drugs seem to attract the worst element of any society, so you will need to protect them and keep quiet about them. *Never* discuss drugs over the radio, meaning don't say something like "Sure, *Yellowbird,* we can spare a couple of Demerol." That suggests to anyone listening in that you have plenty more aboard.

Many cruisers limit the number of prescription drugs to a single broad-spectrum antibiotic and perhaps Lomotil for diarrhea. More than a few cruise without any prescription drugs. Some apparently base this choice on a belief that most conditions requiring drugs other than painkillers are likely to originate ashore, so medical assistance is also likely to be nearby. The first part of this belief is true, but the second part is logically flawed. Much of the best cruising is at the feet of tiny villages where health care may be limited to a monthly visit from a government doctor. Maybe a doctor is only a 50-mile sail away, but that could be against wind and current, the weather could be bad, or the illness aboard could be debilitating.

At least a few cruisers eschew prescription drugs because they believe the likelihood of needing them is lower than the risk of using them inappropriately. Diarrhea—the most common of all traveler's illnesses—provides a good example. Generally speaking, the best treatment is to simply drink lots of liquid, particularly a rehydration salts solution (ORS), and let the illness run its course. But after a day of discomfort, the temptation is to "take something." The most common something is Imodium or Lomotil. Both are effective for simple diarrhea but can complicate a more serious infection, yet they are used with impunity by most sailors if they are among the ship's medical stores.

The physician's credo is "First do no harm." That should be on your mind before you administer or take any prescription drug without consulting a doctor. If you decide to carry a supply of prescription drugs, talk to your doctor about each drug you ask him or her to prescribe, and make notes about uses, dosage, and potential reactions. Many pharmacies now supply a "fact sheet" for each drug. Even if you don't think you would want to "prescribe" a powerful drug for your own patients, keep in mind that you can't follow a doctor's recommendation obtained by radio or telephone if you don't have the drug aboard.

Whether you decide to take a supply of prescription drugs or practice more holistic healing, be sure your medical kit contains most or all of the first-aid supplies listed. The patient can deal with pain in the time-honored way of biting down on a stick, but without sterile bandages, skin closures, and antiseptics, a minor accident can become a major health crisis. Be prepared.

An Ounce of Prevention

Illnesses are generally transmitted in one of three ways—through insect bite, through contaminated food or water, or by contagion. There are exceptions—rabies comes to mind—but the overwhelming majority of illnesses will fall into one of these three categories.

Malaria, dengue fever, yellow fever, encephalitis, and plague, for example, are all transmitted by insect bite. No insect bite, no illness. You need not worry about *any* of these unless they are endemic to the area you are cruising. In the Caribbean, for example, malaria still exists only on the island of Hispaniola (Haiti and Dominican Republic). If you cruise there, your most effective preventative is avoiding insect bite.

Not being ashore all night automatically lowers your risk, but you can reduce it more by wearing sleeves and long pants when you are ashore, especially at dawn and dusk when mosquitoes and sand flies are most active. Treat your clothes with permethrin (Permanone); the repellent effect will last several launderings. Cover all exposed skin fully but sparingly with a repellent containing deet and reapply it about every four hours.

Sand flies may not be deterred by insect repellent, but many cruisers swear Avon's Skin-So-Soft will keep them away. Sand flies are generally more annoyance than health risk, but some species can transmit leishmaniasis.

Screens for all hatches and ports will protect you from insects riding the breeze out to your boat. Some cruisers even enclose cockpits with mosquito netting. As for illnesses transmitted by bugs that don't fly, such as Chagas' disease, not sleeping ashore nearly eliminates exposure.

Among the illnesses transmitted by contaminated food or water are cholera, hepatitis A, dysentery, typhoid fever, and giardiasis, not to mention Montezuma's revenge. Avoid uncooked food and questionable water and you will not be at risk.

Uncooked vegetables are always a risk. If you want a salad, make it yourself, and wash the vegetables thoroughly. Fruits are fine as long as you peel them yourself. Street-vendor food is generally riskier than restaurant fare, but don't be overly influenced by this. Nothing is 100 percent safe, and street-vendor food—often excellent—may be an important part of experiencing a place. Watch out for undercooked meat, fish, and shellfish, no matter who prepares it.

The safest water is rainwater you catch yourself, but almost all sizable communities have a safe water supply. If you have any doubts, treat the water with purification tablets (Potable Aqua) or 2% tincture of iodine—20 drops per gallon of water. Chlorine gives a slightly less reliable result, but if 8 drops per gallon of 4% to 6% chlorine bleach gives the water a slight chlorine odor after 30 minutes, the water will be safe to drink. (No odor, treat it again.) Whether a microfilter will remove *all* harmful microorganisms is unsubstantiated, and charcoal filters only improve the water's taste, so treat dubious water even if you will filter it before use.

For contagious diseases the only shield is vaccination—if a vaccine exists. Check your vaccination status before you go cruising. Most Americans have been immunized against polio. If it has been more than 10 years since your last tetanus shot, get a Td (tetanus and diphtheria) booster. If you were born before 1957 you are likely immune to measles and mumps; otherwise, consider getting an MMR (measles-mumps-rubella) vaccination. Women of childbearing age who have never had an MMR should consider it to immunize themselves against rubella.

Cholera vaccines are only about 50 percent effective, mostly in the first two months after vaccination, and the risk of cholera to U.S. travelers is so low that the CDC (Centers for Disease Control and Prevention), the organization that keeps track of this sort of stuff, doesn't recommend cholera vaccination. Typhoid fever is more widespread, but easy enough to avoid by careful selection of food and drink. Typhoid vaccine can provide some added protection, but like the cholera vaccine, it is only about 50 percent effective. As a practical matter, cruisers rarely get typhoid vaccinations, nor are they vaccinated against encephalitis, unless the cruise will be in parts of Asia where the risk is significant.

Your doctor can test you for susceptibility to hepatitis A. If you are immune, it is one less concern. If you are susceptible, you might want to be vaccinated with immune globulin (IG) if you are going where there is a high endemism. Travelers are at low risk for contracting yellow fever, but if you will be traveling—either by boat or on a side trip—into a yellow-fever-infected area, vaccination will probably be required, and is a good idea anyway.

Vaccines are not available for dengue fever. There is also no vaccine for malaria, and antimalarial drugs (chemoprophylactics) are often ineffective.

For the latest information on vaccination requirements and health risks in countries on your itinerary, thumb through a current travel guide. At least one—the *International Travel Health Guide*—is updated annually. Even more current information is available from the CDC's Internet site at www.cdc.gov.

Despite this litany of global diseases, cruisers as a group are healthier than the residents in your hometown and have a much lower risk of death or disability. Injury, not infection, is the major cause of serious disability or loss of life, and in developed and developing countries alike, the principal cause is motor vehicle crashes. Cruisers are only sporadically exposed to this risk. Statistically, renting motorbikes is particularly dangerous. Walking can also be dangerous in the "Mad Max" traffic environment of some countries. Your momma told you true: "Look both ways."

Tourists also die in fires and drown off the beaches or in the pools of resorts. You are immune from hotel fires, and presumably you have sufficient respect for the water to avoid drowning.

The fact that the medical supply cruisers universally need most often is a Band-Aid speaks volumes about the real health risks of cruising. It isn't remarkable for adhesive strips to be the *only* medical supply used on a cruise. With a little extra care, your first-aid kit may well go untouched for the duration of your cruise.

Poisoning

Unless you have small children aboard, no one is going to be drinking bleach, but cruisers are at increased risk for other types of poisoning.

Ciguatera fish poisoning is the one I most want to call to your attention, because few Americans other than cruisers have even heard of it, despite the fact that it is the most common cause of seafood poisoning in the United States. Toxins found naturally in several kinds of algae sometimes accumulate in reef fish through their diet. If the level of toxicity is high enough, eating the fish can make you sick. The classic symptoms are numbness and tingling around the mouth, sometimes spreading to arms and legs, accompanied by nausea, vomiting, and diarrhea. In severe cases the victim may also experience cardiovascular distress. A signature symptom is hot feeling cold and cold feeling hot. The effects of ciguatera poisoning are rarely serious and usually limited to a few days, but there are isolated cases of symptoms persisting for months and even years.

Most reefs, hence most reef fish, are not ciguatoxic. Ciguatera toxins are accumulative, so the older the fish, the greater the risk. Large barracuda are especially notorious for carrying high levels of toxin, but hogfish, snapper,

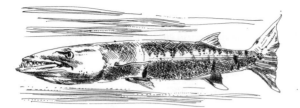

grouper, triggerfish, and jack are also commonly implicated. Ciguatera occurs between latitudes 35° south and north, and outbreaks are localized and sporadic. It is a good idea to inquire if the local fish is safe before you eat it. When no one is around to ask, the safest course is to eat only adolescent (small) fish. Toxin levels are highest in the head and internal organs, so don't eat those if ciguatera could be present.

Ciguatera toxins are unaffected by cooking, marinating, or freezing, and the only reliable test is to feed the fish's liver to the ship's cat—with unpleasant implications for Tabby. If the locals consider the fish safe, it likely is. Pelagic fish like dolphin and tuna don't carry ciguatera.

Improperly canned foods and sometimes contaminated fish are the sources for adult *botulism* poisoning. Because cruisers often can their own foods and have a fish-rich diet, they are statistically in the high-risk group. "High risk" is a relative term, however, since adult botulism affects only about 25 Americans annually.

Botulism is easily avoided with hygienic canning methods strictly followed. It is almost never a problem with canned foods that are cooked before being eaten. Unlike ciguatera, botulism toxins can be destroyed with heat, so if you have any doubts about your canned items, heat them to 15 pounds pressure or boil them for 10 minutes before eating to ensure that they are safe.

Risk from *salmonella* increases on a cruise if you let water limitations, particularly hot water, make you lax in kitchen sanitation. Salmonella thrive on contaminated surfaces, so scrub all dishes and utensils, *and your counter,* with soap and hot water after they have been in contact with raw meat or poultry, *or with raw eggs.* Sanitize the countertop with chlorine bleach—1 teaspoon mixed into a pint of water. For obvious reasons, be sure you also sanitize the sponge or cloth you used to clean the counter.

Leave your wooden cutting board at home, or reserve it for bread. Cut raw meats and poultry on a nonporous acrylic cutting board.

Eggs can be internally contaminated with salmonella, and storing them unrefrigerated lets the number of bacteria grow. This makes raw eggs on a boat riskier than refrigerated ones only a week from the store, but this is of no consequence as long as you cook all eggs thoroughly before eating them.

Limited refrigeration can, however, increase your salmonella risk in another way. Cruisers use all kinds of schemes to avoid refrigerating cooked foods, few with any scientific basis. A common ploy with a pressure cooker is to dip out what you need for a meal, then reseal the cooker and set it aside until the next appropriate meal. Some cruisers continue this cycle for several days. I recommend against this practice, but if you try it, here are the essential precautions.

Sterilize the ladle (stainless steel) by holding it in the flame before you use it to dip food. Reclose the cooker and bring it back up to pressure. The idea here is to essentially "can" the food inside the cooker, but if you don't let the valve rock for a couple of minutes to vent, there is zero chance of creating a sterile vacuum inside the cooker. The truth is there isn't that much chance of maintaining a vacuum anyway because the metal-to-metal seal between the valve and the vent is unlikely to be airtight, and any movement of the boat is sure to make it leak. For subsequent servings, it is essential to bring the cooker back up to full pressure for a couple of minutes. It is the recooking, not the canning, that likely renders this five-day stew "safe" to eat. If it does make you sick, it probably won't kill you.

Salmonellosis is often confused for the flu. If you get diarrhea accompanied by chills, fever, or headache, salmonella is more likely than influenza. Revisit your cleaning and/or cooking practices.

E. coli has been in the news in recent years as the cause of numerous illnesses and a few deaths, particularly among children. Escherichia coli is a common and usually harmless bacteria found in animal intestines (including humans), but one strain designated E. coli O157:H7, produces a powerful toxin. We get it from meat that has been contaminated during slaughter.

Cooking kills this surface bacteria, so there is little risk from a cooked steak or other "slab" meat, even if the interior is rare. Ground meat is another story because the bacteria is distributed throughout the meat. It is imperative to cook ground meat to a center temperature of at least 155°F—until it is no longer pink. Do that—and don't drink unpasteurized milk—and you can scratch E. coli off your health-worry list.

Let's Get Serious

If the worst happens and you do become seriously ill, what then? Seek medical attention. Adequate health care for most common ailments is available in most countries.

In some places virtually all care is distributed from a single hospital or clinic, often government supported. In other places you will find private-practice doctors. Select a doctor to consult the same way that you might select a specialist at home, by asking around. The American embassy or consulate can often be helpful. You might also try the local American Express office.

Absent a life-threatening emergency, consult your own doctor by phone before you undergo any procedures or take any unfamiliar medication. He may not be able to diagnose your problem over the phone, but he can give you an opinion on the treatment.

Don't undergo a transfusion in a foreign country if there is any way to avoid it; blood screening outside the United States is typically less reliable. Fortunately, unexpected transfusions are rarely required except for severe trauma— car crashes—and infrequent gynecological and gastrointestinal emergencies.

In a few countries horrible sanitation and unknown medicine quality renders treatment more dangerous than the ailment. If you need serious medical attention in a country with sub-par medical care, go straight to the airport and fly somewhere else, perhaps home.

The Insurance Quandary

Health insurance in the United States has gotten so expensive that premiums can easily represent 25 to 40 percent of a cruising budget. Stated another way, eliminating the premium can double or triple so-called discretionary dollars, funding restaurants, car rentals, and visits home.

Surveys indicate that most long-term cruisers have no health insurance, or if they do, it is a "catastrophe" policy with a deductible of several thousand dollars. This is not as foolhardy as it may seem, because health care in most parts of the world is relatively inexpensive or even a free government service. Only in America will a serious illness impoverish you if you don't have insurance.

Cruisers in their 20s will view the importance of health insurance differently from cruisers in their 50s. Everyone's situation is unique, and no standard strategy applies. Here, however, are some "rules" for balancing the cost of insurance premiums against the benefits that accrue.

◆ If you don't expect to leave American waters, your need for health insurance is exactly the same while you cruise as it was before.
◆ Even if you are "going foreign," if you state the anticipated duration of your cruise in months, keeping your health insurance in force will be more convenient and perhaps less costly than obtaining new coverage upon your return.
◆ If you expect to be out of the country a year or more, rather than no coverage, consider a policy with a very high deductible—maybe $5,000—and a corresponding low premium. The cost of getting stitches and having bones set still comes out of your pocket, but this

"fixes" your risk at the deductible amount and makes flying home to a health-care system you're familiar with feasible.

If you are thinking about canceling your existing health coverage, be careful if you have ever been diagnosed with any serious problem, even if it no longer exists. Women, for example, who have ever undergone a simple biopsy may find that a new policy with a new insurer broadly excludes all "female" problems. Yes, it is outrageous, but it may be sufficient reason to maintain your existing coverage. If the premium is unmanageable on a cruising budget, maybe you can raise the deductible to reduce it.

If you are insured through an employer, COBRA (Consolidated Omnibus Budget Reconciliation Act of 1985) gives you the right to continue your coverage for up to 18 months by paying the premium. Group policies are often less expensive than individual policies. If your employer has several health-coverage options, evaluate which one best suits cruising and make the appropriate selection before you resign.

What have we left out? If you wear corrective lenses, be sure you take a spare (or spares, in the case of contacts). Also take a copy of the prescription along, just in case. If you have a serious medical condition that could require emergency care, wear an appropriate tag or bracelet.

An emergency bracelet is the perfect analogy for health-related preparation. It is prudent to anticipate illness, but that isn't the same as expecting it. Of all methods of traveling, cruising on your own boat is probably the healthiest. You control the purity of your water, the preparation of your food, the sanitation of your quarters. Take sensible precautions and you are almost assured of fewer health problems afloat than ashore.

11

Taking Care of Your Skin

SAILORS LOVE THE SUN. IT IS RESPONSIBLE FOR THE WIND THAT PUSHES US along. It provides light to see where we're going. It warms the water we swim and dive in. It brightens a rainy afternoon with a rainbow, puts a silver lining on storm clouds. The sun can even tell us exactly where we are on a vast, featureless ocean.

And it gives us cancer.

The Unshaded Truth

This revelation hardly seems a stellar point (no pun intended) in an upbeat book about the joys of cruising, but the unpleasant truth is that the only way you can take up sailing as an occupation and *not* increase your risk of developing skin cancer is if you are already a farmer. Sailor and farmer are the highest-risk occupations.

This does not mean going cruising will give you skin cancer. I am speaking only of *risk*. You can't drive a car, stand up in the bathtub, or make love without a certain degree of risk. And there is such a thing as prevention. That's why we buckle the seat belt, glue rubber flowers on the bottom of the tub, or . . . well, you get the picture. Just because sailors, as a group, run a high risk of skin cancer is no reason you as an individual must also run that risk.

It was among sailors that physicians nearly a century ago first noted the link between the sun and skin cancer. Popularly called "sailor's skin," skin cancer was simply accepted by sailors as part of the job, an occupational hazard no doubt viewed as of little consequence when compared with furling a thrashing sail in the teeth of a gale while standing on a swaying rope 10 stories above the deck. They were wrong about it being of little consequence—dead wrong.

More than 700,000 cases of skin cancer are detected each year in the United States. Fortunately, about 95 percent of them are either basal cell or squamous cell carcinomas. Both occur in the outer layer of skin and are virtually 100 percent curable when treated early.

Skin cancer is relatively easy to detect in its early stage. Tumors most frequently appear as raised translucent pinkish lumps, sometimes with a central depression. Or they may be "heaped-up" sores tending to ulcerate and crust or to ooze. A precursor is red or brown, scaly, sharply outlined patches on the skin, known as actinic keratoses. Any change in the skin, particularly in a mole or wart, can be an early warning.

Basal and squamous cell carcinomas can cause deformities if ignored but are rarely life threatening. The bad boy of skin cancers is malignant melanoma. Melanoma is 12 times more common today than it was 50 years ago. Of all forms of cancer, only lung cancer has shown a greater increase in mortality rate—this in a period of tremendous advances in cancer treatment. This increase in mortality rate despite more effective treatments is occurring because skin cancer is an epidemic. According to epidemiologists, the number

of cases in some areas is doubling each decade. Today in the United States, more than 30,000 cases of melanoma are discovered annually.

How dangerous is melanoma? *Very* dangerous. Only 65 percent of those who contract malignant melanoma survive five years. It is a hell of a price for a "nice" tan.

You, Me, and UV

The link between sun exposure and skin cancer is so widely known that one might expect lying in the sun to be taboo, but a trip to the beach or a look around any anchorage where boats gather suggests otherwise. Our cultural obsession with tanning is greatly responsible for the rampant increase in skin cancer. While sailors are no more obsessed than secretaries, sailors do have a greater opportunity to indulge that compulsion.

Catching a few rays doesn't automatically mean that down the road you'll develop skin cancer. In fact, just a little effort can almost eliminate the risk, although if you are a redhead with freckles; blond, blue-eyed, and fair; or otherwise prone to sunburn easily, you will have to be particularly diligent.

The most damaging component of sunlight is in the ultraviolet spectrum. Fortunately the ozone layer in the stratosphere screens out most UV radiation, but what does make it through is potentially harmful. Many scientist believe a depletion of the ozone level caused by industrial chemicals has also contributed to the skin-cancer epidemic.

The UV spectrum is divided into UVA, the so-called "cool" rays, and UVB, the "hot" ones (and UVC, which is screened out by the atmosphere). UVB has long been singled out as harmful, UVA relatively safe, but recent research reveals that at the very least UVA damages collagen and may also play a role in cancer. The prudent course is to consider *all* UV radiation potentially harmful.

When UV light strikes the skin, the skin recognizes the danger and begins a two-step process to protect itself. First, the pigment already present in the skin's upper layers begins to darken—the process we call tanning. Second, the pigment-producing cells located in the lower layers are stimulated to produce new melanin (pigment), which migrates to the surface, yielding a darker tan and additional protection from the sun. The first step is apparent in a matter of hours, but this initial "blush" provides only a small amount of protection. New melanin granules are the skin's big guns, but it takes almost two days after initial exposure for melanin production to begin, *two weeks* before maximum protection is achieved.

Both squamous cell and basal cell carcinomas are associated with *prolonged* exposure to UV radiation and generally occur after years of exposure— the so-called sailor's skin. Melanoma, on the other hand, is more often related to brief exposures of *high doses* of UV radiation. A blistering sunburn, aside from the immediate discomfort, makes you a candidate for melanoma. It is high-risk carelessness. The good news—at least for the potential cruiser—is that a single day at the beach is probably more dangerous than a year on the boat.

Photoaging

The risk of cancer is not the only reason to limit your skin's exposure to the sun. When the sun's rays are powerful enough, they penetrate through the top layer—the epidermis—to the dermis below. There the radiation, including apparently UVA, damages collagen fibers and blocks production of new ones.

It is collagen fibers that make the skin cling to the body. As we grow old, collagen production lessens naturally, and our once perfectly fitted birthday suit begins to sag and wrinkle. Collagen damage by the sun, called *photoaging*, brings on this condition prematurely.

Don't miss the irony here: sun worshipers, those seeking the body beautiful by spending hours sunbathing, are destroying the very thing they are trying to enhance. I think Coco Chanel says it best: "Nature is responsible for the face you have at 20. You are responsible for the face you have at 50."

Say Eye

Excessive sun exposure can also harm your eyes. A bright day in snow country can leave a skier with a severely sunburned cornea—*snow blindness*. While there is usually less reflected light on the water, every tropical sailor has experienced a white-sky day when the light reflected off thin, high clouds is painful. Pain is your body's alarm system.

A study of 800 Chesapeake Bay fishermen revealed that those with the most sun exposure were three times more likely to develop cataracts than those with the least exposure. A million Americans per year develop cataracts. *Macular degeneration,* an eye disorder that is a major cause of blindness, probably isn't caused by sunlight, but both UV and deep-blue visible light are now suspected as aggravating factors.

Okay, enough gloom and doom. It is so easy to avoid the harmful effects of the sun that these problems should not be so prevalent in our society. All that is required is an awareness of the risks, and diligence in limiting exposure—in both senses of the word.

Let's start with protecting your eyes. If you are in the sun long enough to affect your skin, you should be wearing sunglasses. It is simply not true that sunglasses cause your eyes to dilate and admit more UV radiation. Even cheap drugstore sunglasses typically screen out 70 percent or more of UVB. Glasses labeled "ANSI Z80.3 General Purpose UV Requirements" block at least 95 percent of the UVB and 60 percent of UVA and visible light. A "Special Purpose UV Requirements" label means the glasses block out more than 99 percent of UVB. These are your best choice.

For use on the water, sunglasses should block more than 60 percent of the visible light—75 percent is better. If the glasses aren't labeled, check them by looking at yourself in a mirror; you shouldn't be able to see your eyes.

Blue light is suspected of causing retina damage by some scientists, pooh-poohed by others, but glasses that block 75 percent of visible light shield your eyes from a significant amount of blue light. Amber and brown lenses are the best blue blockers.

Be sure the lenses in your sunglasses are polarized. While the water is probably murky where you live, it is likely to be clear where you cruise. Polarized sunglasses eliminate surface glare and allow you to look into the water to determine depth and see underwater hazards. Polarized lenses are *essential* cruising gear. You can get polarized lenses in your prescription sunglasses.

Don't buy gradient lenses—the ones that are dark on the top and nearly clear at the bottom—for use on the boat. They offer little or no protection from the considerable amounts of light reflected from the water and the deck.

You get the most eye protection from a wraparound style, but it is more important to buy a style you like and that feels comfortable enough to wear for hours at a time. If you don't have them on, it is irrelevant how good they are.

The Satin Pillbox Is Out

Unless you are bald, the most sun-abused part of your body is your face. Particularly vulnerable to the sun's assault are your less vertical features—the nose, the top of the ears, the cheeks, and the lower lip. Protect your vulnerable face with a *proper* hat, not a visor or cap, which leave ears, neck, and cheeks exposed. You don't like hats? Consider this: studies have shown that wearing a hat with a 3-inch all-around brim reduces the incidence of skin cancer by about 70 percent.

The most dangerous part of the day, in the sense of amount of UV exposure, is between 10 a.m. and 2 p.m. Staying out of the midday sun is the first and best line of defense, but when you can't do that, wear a hat with a 10-to-2 brim. If your hat shades only your lower lip from 11:30 A.M. to 12:30 P.M., you need a different hat.

Because the UVB level is still at about 85 percent as late as 3:30, 60 percent at 4, even a broad-brimmed hat leaves your neck and lower lip exposed. If your hair isn't long, outfit your hat with a neck curtain. Some cruisers resort to wearing a bandanna or a surgical mask to shade their lips if facing the afternoon sun. When on one cruise I carelessly let my lower lip burn, for a few

days I wore a visor pulled down below my eyes. I looked like a duck, but my lip stayed in the shade.

Besides shading your horizontal features, a wide hat brim provides added UV protection for your eyes. If you choose a straw hat, don't pick one with an open-weave brim. A cruising hat needs to be functional first, then fashionable. And don't leave without a hat, planning on picking one up in the island straw markets when you get south. You will *need* a hat long before then. The straw market is where you buy a *new* hat.

Long Sleeves Are In

Your best protection from UV rays is clothing. If you tan smart (read "slowly"), your skin develops its own protection from the sun, and after it does you can wear your bikini or your thong or even less. Meanwhile, covering up is the order of the day.

Covering up means long pants and long sleeves. Loose-fitting, tight-weave cotton provides both the most protection and the most comfort. Skip loose-weave items; if they let the sun through, they aren't protecting you. Dark colors shield better, but in the tropics light colors and whites will be much cooler.

Wearing a T-shirt while swimming and snorkeling is not as protective as you might think. A dry cotton T-shirt typically offers only about one-third the protection of SPF 15 sunscreen. When wet it is as transparent to UV radiation as it is to lecherous eyes. While synthetics like Dacron are less transparent when wet, they are a poor barrier to UV to begin with. A thick cotton shirt is better, and this is where a dark color is a good choice.

Even after your skin has developed a rich tan, do it a favor and wear sleeves and pants in the middle of the day. Your skin can muster only so much natural protection. It is counting on your brain for a little help.

Shade in a Tube

Another way of saving your skin from damage is by using a sunscreen. The reason I didn't earlier list sunscreen among the medicine chest contents is because it belongs out in the open—on a shelf right by the companionway—so everyone aboard will slop some on before leaving the cabin.

Regardless of manufacturer, sunscreens designate a sun protection factor (SPF) based on a scale determined by the Food and Drug Administration. This number, 2 through 50, is supposed to represent the relative amount of time it will take to get the same dose of UVB radiation when wearing the screen compared to when not wearing it. For example, if you wear an SPF 2 sunscreen, it will take twice as long to get the same dose of UVB as without the screen. Wearing SPF 15, you can stay in the sun 15 times as long as without it. The SPF designation doesn't tell you anything about UVA protection, but most SPF 15 and above sunscreens filter out at least two-thirds of UVA. Some block it all. Read the label.

Products with an SPF of 15 or above are usually called sun*blocks,* but they don't do what their name implies. You will still tan wearing SPF 15, but at a much safer pace. Considering how often you will be in the sun while cruising, there is no reason to use anything below SPF 15.

Sunscreen manufacturers try to lure customers with ever higher SPF numbers, but you should know that because of diminishing returns, most dermatologists consider SPF 15 adequate. An SPF 15 sunscreen filters out more than 93 percent of UVB. SPF 30 filters out just under 97 percent, hardly a significant improvement. However, the tests behind SPF numbers assume a generous application—about a quarter of a 4-ounce bottle. Since most of us actually apply less than half that amount, we get only an SPF 7 protection from an SPF 15 product. A real-world application of SPF 30 sunscreen should still provide the SPF 15 protection level cancer experts recommend.

"Waterproof" on the label means that the sunscreen should still work after 80 minutes of immersion, but some sunscreens provide six to eight hours of protection from a single application, even if you spend all that time in the water. This is the best kind of sunscreen for a cruise.

PABA is gone as an ingredient, so sunscreens rarely cause the skin irritation they did a few years ago. (Test a sunscreen by applying it to the inside of your upper arm and leaving it for 24 hours.) Sunscreens come in sprays, lotions, gels, and cool-feeling alcohol-based formulas, so you should be able to find one you can wear comfortably; it is no good to you in the bottle. Try two or three different brands before you settle on one to stock up on.

The best application strategy is to apply sunscreen *before* you get dressed, so your whole body is protected. Don't quit using it when you have a tan. The best protection the body can muster naturally is about SPF 4, so if you don't help it, your skin will be accumulating damage.

To protect lips, you need a product that contains wax to keep the screen in place. Women have the attractive option of buying a sunscreen lipstick such as Clinique Sun Buffer. Because the lips have no natural protection—they don't contain melanin—you need a high SPF, at least 15. Be sure the SPF number is on the label; lip products that just say "contains sunscreen" can have SPFs as low as 2.

For a complete sunblock for your nose and lips, put a tube of zinc oxide aboard. It is ugly, but nothing works better.

Soft and Silky

Hair is also susceptible to damage from the sun. A number of "hair sunscreens" are on the market. These products do provide some protection from the sun's radiation, but their main ingredient is a conditioning cream. Liberal use of a deep conditioner is really the only secret to keeping your hair healthy on a boat. Conditioning *before* you go in the ocean helps to protect your hair from the drying effects of salt water.

The very best protection for your hair is a hat, the very one you're already planning to wear to protect your face and your eyes.

Awnings—Don't Leave Home Without Them

Whenever I was being unusually stupid, I can remember my mom telling me that I "didn't have sense enough to come in out of the rain." Altering the last word to "sun" doesn't change the message a bit. Sitting out in the sun day after day subjects you to enormous doses of radiation, yet each year an astounding number of cruisers set out without an awning. While you might get along just fine without a sun awning on a cruise up to Maine and Nova Scotia or gunkholing in Puget Sound, if your cruise is taking you toward the tropics, a harbor awning is essential equipment.

But don't expect too much from your awning. While awning shade is certainly preferable to direct sunlight, it won't protect you from an overdose of UV, particularly during those lily-white early days. UV comes at you from all directions on the water, the ripples acting like a million tiny mirrors. The typically white deck reflects plenty of sunlight as well.

Whether you make your own awning or have it made, there are a few things you should know. *Never* make an awning out of Dacron sailcloth; UV radiation passes right through it. Polypropylene tarpaulins—those shiny bright blue or green plastic-looking things—are sometimes used as an awning because they're cheap (and ready-made). The sun protection is okay, but the noise such awnings make in a breeze is unbearable. Even if you can stand it, the boats anchored near you won't like it very much.

Boatowners often select acrylic canvas (Sunbrella) for a harbor awning because they want it to match the other canvas on the boat. Acrylic canvas is an excellent awning material: it provides good UV protection, resists sun damage, and doesn't rot or mildew. The only serious drawback, other than relatively high cost, is color. Air temperature beneath a dark blue awning in the tropics will be at least 20°F higher than beneath a white awning. Forget about matching the canvas; chose white or a light color.

Natural canvas, treated to resist mildew, is another good awning fabric. At about half the price of acrylic canvas, treated natural canvas (Sunforger) wears better, provides excellent sun protection, and is naturally waterproof.

Because an awning is essentially a flat sheet of canvas with grommets in the corners, many cruisers make their own. If you decide to give awning construction a try, you will find that design is more difficult than construction. In its simplest form, a harbor awning is draped over the boom like a tent, and the corners are tied down to the lifelines. A variation on this basic design is

the addition of battens or awning poles to hold the sides high. More complex awnings can have hoist points to get the awning higher above the deck, and snap- or zip-on side panels to keep out early-morning and late-afternoon sun.

A sailing awning, often called a *Bimini top,* provides welcome shade while underway, but Biminis are typically too small to serve as the boat's only awning. Nevertheless a Bimini top is a good addition to a cruising boat going far south.

Another Nasty Blow

Although less dangerous than sunburn, windburn can be painful and damaging to your skin. On a bright day a breeze not only masks the heat that normally warns us our skin is burning, it actually accelerates the damage caused by the sun. Even without the sun, wind assaults the surface of your skin, particularly your face, and leaves it dry and damaged.

Mountain climbers and arctic explorers protect their faces with ski masks and goggles, but try shielding your face this way in the tropics and you'll either be committed or arrested. The trick to windburn protection is to keep your skin moist. A thin coat of petroleum jelly can act as both a barrier and a moisturizer, but remember that it provides no UV protection. Put on your sunscreen first. Some sunscreens include moisturizers, but for a long day on the water in 20 knots of wind, they may need some help.

The most effective preventative is to stay out of the wind. When we installed a dodger on our boat, not only did it keep cold ocean spray out of the cockpit, it shielded us as well from the assault of the wind—even on windy days at anchor. The almost constant battle against windburn became a thing of the past.

If your cruising budget can afford a spray dodger, install one. Be sure that the clear front panel can be unzipped and rolled up or removed. When the wind drops you want every puff of breeze to have an unimpeded path across the cockpit.

Sunshine Might Save Your Life

Here is good news. Colon cancer is nearly nonexistent at the equator, its prevalence increasing with the latitude. Breast cancer seems to follow a similar pattern. A number of studies have led many scientists to conclude that both colon and breast cancers are directly related to a vitamin D deficiency.

Vitamin D is the "sunshine vitamin." A cruise to lower latitudes is sure to increase your vitamin D intake, both because the level of solar radiation will be higher and because you will be spending considerably more time in the sun. Studies have shown that higher levels of vitamin D reduce the likelihood of colon cancer by as much as two-thirds, with the implication that it may have a similar effect on breast cancer risk.

Doctors trying to understand the "why" believe it may be because higher calcium levels seem to prevent uncontrolled cell growth, and vitamin D helps the body absorb calcium. Additional calcium has other benefits, most notably strengthening bones. Postmenopausal women in particular need additional calcium to ward off osteoporosis, and sunlight clearly helps.

Concerns about skin cancer, legitimate though they are, can make us forget that the sun also gives life to virtually everything on the planet. Who doesn't feel their mood improve when gray skies give way to sunlight? Intuitively we know that regular doses of sunlight must be healthy, and scientific studies confirm that.

Moisturizing—Inside and Out

More good news. Seawater is much easier on your skin than the chlorinated water of a swimming pool. The salt residue, however, can be drying, so after a saltwater swim, give yourself a freshwater rinse. Then rub a little baby oil on your skin, but *not* if you are going to leave your skin exposed to the sun—you want to lubricate it, not fry it.

Don't neglect moisturizing your skin from the inside. Aside from all the benefits to the rest of your system, drinking plenty of water is great for your skin, helping to replace moisture lost to perspiration. Two quarts of liquid a day—water, tea, juices, but not booze—is not too much.

When you are in the grip of a northern winter, the tropical sun seems like a miracle cure. The sun can indeed be medicinal, but like every other drug, it can also be dangerous. Safety is simply a matter of limiting dosage.

We can sum up all you need to do to protect your skin from the sun with a slogan the Aussies have long used in anti-skin-cancer campaigns Down Under: SLIP! SLOP! SLAP!

It means "Slip on a shirt. Slop on some sunscreen. Slap on a hat."

It is a slogan to live by.

12

Cleanliness

NOT EVERYONE HAS AN EQUAL APPRECIATION FOR THE VALUE OF PERSONAL hygiene. I am sorry to report that more than a few cruisers have a much closer resemblance to vagrants than to yachtsmen. I find this species of dirtbag particularly reprehensible, especially in pristine cruising areas where a bucket over the side fetches an endless supply of cleansing water. Such boat bums are dirty not because they lack the facilities to stay clean but because they lack the desire.

It is true that few cruising boats are equipped with washers and dryers, bathtubs are as common as pianos, onboard showers are tiny, fresh water is limited, and hot water is mostly nonexistent. However, these limitations do not require cruising sailors to give up cleanliness; they simply require a different approach.

As a dedicated aficionado of the long, lingering shower, when I first started cruising I looked forward to marina stops mostly—often solely—for

the shower facilities they provided. Never mind that they were never clean, the water was often brackish, and they *never* had hot water. I turned the handle and water gushed—or sometimes dribbled—out of a real showerhead and coursed over my body until I turned it off again. Ahh, such luxury.

The fact that these public showers were far-too-often infinitely dirtier than I was eventually had me questioning my patronage. Today more marinas pay more attention to the condition of their shower facilities, but not before we developed a number of simple strategies to allow us to handle all bathing on the boat.

Showering Solutions

Sales representatives are quick to point out the spacious shower enclosure in their new Takeuaway 37, but they don't mention the 100-gallon water capacity. A five-minute shower takes 15 to 20 gallons. You do the math.

Here is another equation. Water can be expensive in island countries without groundwater. In the Bahamas, for example, marinas typically charge 40 cents a gallon for desalinated water. That makes a five-minute shower cost $8. Ouch!

You can install a full-size bathtub or a shower stall big enough to echo and you still won't be able to duplicate shoreside bathing habits. The problem is the size of the tanks, not the size of the head. A 30-foot cruising boat may carry only 60 to 80 gallons of fresh water in its tanks. Even a 45-footer is unlikely to carry much more than 200 gallons.

Here, in the order of the effort they require, are four strategies for dealing with the reality of a limited freshwater supply:

- ◆ *Conservation.* The easiest way to stretch your water supply is to use only the amount needed. Never let the water run while you lather or brush your teeth. Better yet, limit pressure water to the shower only, installing manual foot pumps at all basins to allow precise water delivery.

  Use only a handheld showerhead with a fingertip shutoff so all the water strikes your body and you can stop the flow instantly. A sprayer with a spring-loaded shutoff intended for a kitchen sink makes an excellent boat showerhead. Install a flow-restricting washer at the hose connection; the lesser flow rate is not as satisfying while you are showering, but the effect—a clean body— is exactly the same with far less water consumption.

  Some cruisers carry shower conservation one step further, using a pump garden sprayer for showering. The spray head delivers a fine mist that provides an efficient shower using an amazingly small amount of water, typically less than a quart. If you are skeptical, consider how you clean windows and counters, not by flooding them but by spritzing and toweling them off. You can clean skin the same way just as effectively. Try it before you snub it; at the very least you will use the sprayer to give yourself a miserly, salt-removing freshwater rinse after swimming.

Reduce freshwater consumption by substituting seawater at every opportunity. If the water outside is clean enough to swim in, it is clean enough for all dishwashing. (If you don't already have a sea-water spigot in the galley, have one installed before you go cruising.) Seawater often is even clean enough for cooking. Boil eggs or steam vegetables with it. A cup of seawater has approximately 2 teaspoons of salt in it, so instead of adding the called-for tablespoon of salt when boiling pasta, for example, substitute a cup and a half of sea-water, conserving an equivalent amount of fresh water. It adds up.

Take a tub of waterless hand cleaner (GoJo), available from hard-ware and auto-supply stores. It will save gallons of water when the onboard mechanic emerges from the engine room with grease up to his elbows. Cleansing cream also cruises well, exceptionally effective at removing dried-on salt spray from the face and gentler to the skin than soap.

◆ *Rain collection.* In many parts of the world, and particularly in the tropics, enough rain will regularly fall *on your boat* to more than meet all your freshwater needs. A half inch of rainfall drops nearly 100 gal-lons of water on the deck of a 35-foot boat. All you have to do is catch it and get it into your tanks. This can be as simple as plugging the scuppers and opening the on-deck fill cap to let the water run into the tank rather than over the side. Since we fish and walk and clean conch on the deck, Olga and I have never been comfortable with this method aboard our boat, but many cruisers prefer it to all other catchment schemes. Let the rain rinse away salt deposits and all other contaminants for a few minutes before you plug the scuppers.

A compromise is to "fence" the cabintop with low molding to catch the rain and direct it into a hose leading to the tank. The cab-intop sees less traffic than the rest of the deck and is less likely to contaminate the runoff.

We prefer to let the harbor awning do double duty as a rain catchment. This requires a well-rigged awning because rainstorms are often accompanied by wind. A harbor awning that you have to take off every time the wind pipes up is a nuisance anyway, so once you have a good awning design for your boat, using it to catch water requires nothing more than installing drains of some sort in the low spot(s) of the awning. Some designs incorporate a canvas gutter along the outboard edges. During an average month in the relatively dry Bahamas, a 15 × 10 awning can funnel close to 500 gallons of sweet water into your tanks.

◆ *Adding capacity.* Installing additional water tanks reduces the available stowage space for other items, and full tanks add substantial weight. Still, additional tankage can be a worthwhile addition if it (they) can be installed low in the boat, particularly in bilge areas unsuitable for most other stowage. Tanks installed in the ends of a boat may give the boat an uncomfortable motion at sea, at least until they are empty. Water weighs about 8 pounds per gallon, so installing a tank under a settee can give your boat an annoying list.

If you decide to add a water tank, a rigid tank is less susceptible to chafe and leakage than a flexible one. Flex tanks, however, will conform to an odd-shaped space. Having a loose flex tank aboard can let you take advantage of a generous downpour when the ship's tanks are already full. A flex tank in the dinghy can also serve as a kind of minitanker. Jugs do the same thing, but where water is available at a dock or seawall, the tank is easier. Back at your anchored boat you pump the load into the ship's tanks without ever lifting anything.

Cruising boats too often carry extra water (and fuel) in 5-gallon jugs lashed on deck. Although compromises are sometimes required, particularly on smaller boats, it is hard to imagine a worse place to carry water underway. At anchor, however, on-deck jugs provide a convenient sun-warmed water supply for a deck shower.

◆ *Watermakers.* It is possible to convert seawater to drinking water by forcing it through a special membrane, a very fine filter that lets the water molecules pass but not the salt. Reverse-osmosis desalinators are common aboard large motoryachts, and more and more are finding their way aboard more modest cruising boats.

The obvious advantage of a watermaker is that it can make you completely independent of local water supplies, and if the watermaker has high enough capacity, it can obviate the need for any water conservation. It is the only option that has the potential to allow as many lingering showers aboard as you please regardless of weather.

You want one, right? Not so fast. A small unit capable of producing just 6 gallons per hour costs about $4,000, and the prices go up from there. Large units are directly driven by the engine or require a 110-volt (or 220) auxiliary generator, but even a small 12-volt watermaker draws so much power that the engine needs to be running while it is in use. Why am I telling you this?

Let's say you plan to run the engine an hour a day to pull down the freezer and charge the batteries. If you also run the watermaker, you will get 6 gallons of water—hardly enough for that long shower you're after. Over a six-month cruise, you will make only a little more than 1,000 gallons. That makes the desalinated water cost you $4 a gallon. Double ouch!

If you want a five-minute shower every day, you need to run the desalinator 3½ hours, meaning run the engine that long each day. With the fuel cost of the extra engine time—say $2 a day—the per-gallon cost drops to about $1.20 per gallon, making your 20-gallon shower cost $24 a day. And who can stand to listen to the engine for 3½ hours?

The longer your cruise, the lower the per-gallon cost of a watermaker. And the more you run your engine for other purposes—like moving the boat—the lower the water cost. But even over a two-year cruise making 20 gallons every day, the water will still cost you 27 cents a gallon just for the cost of the equipment. Per-shower cost: $5.40.

Bigger desalinators have a lower per-gallon cost to operate, but only if you can make use of their extra capacity. If, for example, you run a $6,000, 12.5-gallon-per-hour unit all the time, making 300 gallons a day with it, the one-year cost, including fuel cost (but not engine wear), is almost $15,000 or about 13.5 cents a gallon. If you use the same system to make just 20 gallons a day—while you run the refrigeration system—the out-of-pocket cost is only the price of the unit (plus maintenance), but the per-gallon cost balloons to 82 cents a gallon.

The bottom line on watermakers is the bottom line. They are expensive to buy, complicated and not always trouble-free, and they require long engine hours to produce significant volume. And they have no use when you return home—where all the water you want is free at your dock.

Seawater Bathing

For warm-weather cruising you can use seawater for most of your bathing needs. If you are swimming and diving every day, you are also soaking off dirt and grime. Dishwashing detergents, particularly Joy and Dawn, and most shampoos lather well in salt water, so use a squirt at the end of your last swim of the day and you will be squeaky clean.

Well, maybe not squeaky; salt water leaves you feeling sticky, and if you leave the salt on your body, it harbors moisture and attracts various fungi. In the tropics it can promote all kinds of skin disorders. You can get most of the salt off with immediate and vigorous toweling, but a quick freshwater rinse removes all of it and leaves your skin as clean as a long soak in a tub. And it leaves your towel salt-free.

For days when you don't swim you can still pour buckets of seawater over yourself. Saltwater bathing is even easier if you have a deck-wash hose. Equipping your boat for pressure seawater on deck is easy and inexpensive— around $100—and with it you can shower as long as you like for only the cost of the fraction of an amp-hour the pump will draw. The same pump can supply a saltwater spray head below deck, or you can simply run the hose into the head through a hatch, but you will have to be meticulous about wiping the shower down or it will soon be a mildew garden. A curtain enclosure for the deck may ultimately prove more sensible.

Use conditioner in your hair to keep it soft. Some cruisers also add a capful of fabric softener to a bucketful of water for the final saltwater rinse, before the conditioner and freshwater rinse. As previously mentioned, putting conditioner in your hair *before* you swim will protect it from drying out and make it soft.

For an after-swim freshwater rinse, a pump garden sprayer is hard to beat for efficiency and frugality. Giving it a longer hose will make it much more convenient to use. Left sitting in the sun, a garden sprayer can also provide a hot shower. Alternatively you can rig a "telephone" shower on deck, fed from your pressure water system. When weather permits, showering on deck eliminates a lot of dampness below.

Don't overlook the value of talcum powder. Olga and I take a huge container and use it liberally. It is as soothing to your skin as to a baby's and likewise helps keep you dry. Sitting on a boat in the tropics is not the same as sitting in an air-conditioned office. Your tush will appreciate the help, trust me.

Cruising Coiffure

Female cruisers can often tolerate months away from a hair salon, but men soon look like castaways. Not only does unkempt hair look unattractive, it can interfere with local acceptance. And, in the tropics, long hair is hot—regardless of gender.

Keeping hair and beards trimmed on a boat is not that difficult. Battery-powered clippers cost less than $20, and with a little practice, anyone can do a professional-looking job. Electric clippers can't be beat for trimming a beard, but I prefer a comb-style razor trimmer for cutting hair. Pharmacies sell them for about $5.

A comb and scissors will also do the job and is the best choice for styling and keeping long hair trimmed. Go to a beauty supply and buy a good pair of hair-cutting shears. This is also a good time to get a small pair of scissors for mustache trimming.

To avoid hair all over the boat, haircuts are best done on the beach. Wait until you are alone if you don't want other cruisers lined up for their turn in the chair. On the other hand, a couple of hours practicing your barbering skill on fellow cruisers can be bartered for mechanical help, canvaswork, or what-need-you. And you will be doing *all* cruisers a service, if you take my meaning.

A cruise can be an opportunity to try a new look. If you hate it, it will grow out before you get back. You are likely to be happiest with a style that is cool and easy to care for. When you get down-island, you might even give beaded braids a try.

Washer and Dryer

Keeping clothes clean on a boat is a bigger challenge than keeping bodies clean. There is no workable substitute for submerging clothes and agitating them to get them clean, then rinsing thoroughly to get out all the detergent. This process takes a significant amount of water.

Most cruisers try to do laundry ashore. In the United States, if a marina doesn't provide washers and dryers you will surely find a laundromat nearby, but laundry facilities are harder to come by in many other countries. If you do find one, it may not be the godsend you imagine. Hot water? Forget about it. Brackish water is more likely, which means your "clean" clothes won't completely dry. We've seen 20-washer laundromats with only one washer working. Water pressures are often so low that the attendant has to supplement the fill cycle with a couple of equally anemic garden hoses. You can imagine how effective the rinse cycle must be.

In fairness we have also come across ice-cold air-conditioned laundromats featuring popcorn machines and cable TV, but good facilities are the exception. Today we keep an eye out for good laundry facilities, and when we run across one, we take full advantage, giving almost everything aboard a machine wash. Between laundromats, we do the laundry aboard and, like many other cruisers, have found it to be less chore and more therapy.

You need ample fresh water to do laundry. *Never use salt water.* If you leave the salt in the fabric, the clothes will be stiff and irritating and never dry. You *must* rinse all salt out of the clothes, and the amount of extra fresh water required to do that will exceed the amount you would have used to wash the clothes in fresh water to begin with.

Where does all this fresh water come from? Laundry day is often determined for us by the weather. After a rain shower, we often have plenty of water unsuitable for our tanks, but perfect for washing. Here is how. Keep the interior of the dinghy fuel-free and wipe it down occasionally to remove salt encrustation, and it becomes the perfect rain catchment for laundry water. Just ¼ inch of rain puts 5 gallons of fresh water into our 8-foot dinghy. Instead of bailing it over the side, we pump it into a jug, and it gives us plenty of water for laundry. Also while we let the first few minutes of rain rinse our catchment awning, we save the runoff for laundry rather than letting it run into the sea. A dark-colored jug on deck can provide warmer wash water than you will find in many laundromats.

When it doesn't rain, you may have to get extra fresh water from shore to do laundry. Some cruisers take the laundry to the water supply, turning a dock, a quay, or even the area around the community faucet into their personal laundry facility. Please! Aside from how disrespectful of the local residents this is, it is so much easier to transport water.

Washing styles vary. Some cruisers put laundry in a bucket and use a toilet plunger to agitate it—like churning butter. Others carry a child's inflatable wading pool as a convenient large basin and work the clothes and linens by hand. Still others carry an old-fashioned corrugated washboard or a soft nylon brush for scrubbing. Personally, I'm a soaker, preferring to let the water and the detergent do most of the work. I typically leave the laundry in the wash water about two hours, agitating it about every half hour. Stains get special attention, but normal grime and perspiration soak out well. For more agitating action, try floating a lidded bucket with the bail tied tight at the bow; wave action keeps the bucket, and the clothes inside, in motion.

By the way, liquid laundry detergents are better than powders for the damp environment of a boat, and they mix more easily. Use about a third of a capful to a gallon of water. If fresh water is limited, cut the soap amount in half. The clothes will still come clean, and you will be able to get away with a single rinse.

The secret to effective rinsing is to wring as much soapy water out of the fabric as possible before putting the item into the rinse water. Clothes are easy, but linens and towels are harder to wring out effectively. Try looping them around a clean stanchion, putting the ends together, then twisting. This lets you apply approximately twice the force. In foreign hardware stores you may run across a clamp-on hand-crank wringer—like the one Great-Grandma had on her old four-legged Maytag, but smaller. Wringers squeeze most of the soap out of clothes and are much easier on the fabric than twisting, so one could be a good addition to your cruising equipment.

When the clothes are well wrung, put them into a bucket of clean fresh water to rinse. The addition of a little softener will aid in soap removal, give the clothes a pleasant scent, and leave them softer when they dry. If you prefer it, ½ cup of vinegar substituted for the softener will do essentially the same things. Wring out each piece thoroughly, then give all a second rinse in fresh water. Wring them out again (you see how nice a wringer would be) and hang them out to dry.

Lifelines make fine clotheslines, but wipe them free of salt before you drape your clean clothes over them. You will need plenty of clothespins, particularly in the trade winds. Sheets can be hung from the rigging—like flags—but we usually spread ours over the awning, clipping them securely at the front.

Hang out clothes carefully and they generally dry with few wrinkles, particularly blends. If you have a lot of 100 percent cotton items aboard and you plan to wear them ashore, you may want to touch them up with an iron. A travel iron is worthless on a boat unless you spend a lot of time plugged into shore, but a small flatiron picked up from a junk shop can be heated on the stove. You won't use it that often.

Don't Forget the Hamper

Like a garbage container, a dirty-clothes hamper is a cruising essential but rarely a standard boat feature. And when a hamper is provided, too often it is a solid bin. Hampers have to breathe. A clothes hamper is perhaps best located in the head, where you are already waging a war against odor. Any contribution there from dirty socks will be inconsequential.

Front-opening hampers are common, but if you are building a hamper, make it top-opening if you can. With a top-opening hamper the net bag—for breathability—can envelope *all* the space immediately beneath the vanity top. When the bag is long and wide, it doesn't need to extend very far down into the locker. Such a hamper makes effective use of space that is otherwise almost certainly wasted.

A stick-up on the underside of the lid will combat odors, and it is also a good idea to give the contents of the hamper an occasional shot of Lysol to prevent mildew. Let clothes dry before you put them in the hamper, and never include saltwater-wetted items, such as swim towels. We normally keep swim towels on deck. When we retire them, they go into a net bag hanging in a cockpit locker.

On the subject of cross contamination, never put clothes you have worn back with your clean items. If you plan to rewear a garment before it goes into the laundry—everybody does—find an airy place to keep it until you want it again.

Keeping House

Housekeeping on a boat is much less demanding than keeping a 3/2 ranch-style clean. Because of your surroundings, dusting is rarely required. There is no carpet to vacuum and precious little floor to mop. Food crumbs and sand are the main cleaning problems.

A whisk broom and a dust bin may be the only housecleaning equipment you need. Get a soft-bristle hand broom—not the straw kind. A 6-inch paintbrush is an effective substitute.

A 12-volt vacuum cleaner intended for car interiors is very handy on a boat. I am happy to recommend the Black & Decker CarVac. These units are inexpensive, powerful enough to suck sand, salt, and crumbs from crevices and cushion covers, don't present a stowage problem, and last for decades.

Clean plastic laminate surfaces in the boat the same way you do at home. Use your favorite furniture polish (Pledge) on varnished wood surfaces. Feed bare wood with lemon oil. A towel will be better than a mop for cleaning the cabin sole.

A Head Examination

More often than not, marine toilets stink. At a boat show Olga and I recently attended, even the head compartments in several display boats reeked. Yours doesn't have to.

Start with the toilet. It can't leak anywhere or it will smell. Run your fingers over every inch of the pump assembly—I know, I'm sorry, but it's the only way—and if you find any dampness, the head must be rebuilt. Some cheap models simply cannot be made leak free around the pump shaft. You will never regret replacing it with a good head such as Groco's Model K or Wilcox Crittenden's Skipper.

Next check the hose, particularly the discharge hose. This is the most common source of unpleasant odors. Regular hose allows odors inside to permeate right through the wall. Check it by wiping the discharge hose vigorously with a damp cloth, then—I'm sorry—put your nose close to the cloth and sniff. A hint of odor condemns the hose. Replacement hose should specify that it is odor-proof "sanitary" hose, but it is a good idea to check it anyway after the toilet has been in service for a while. You can minimize discharge-hose problems by using PVC pipe—household plumbing—for most of the discharge run, with short hose "cuffs" at each end to keep the necessary flexibility in the installation.

Be sure all hoses have dual clamps where they attach to the toilet and to other fittings. This is primarily a safety measure, but dual clamps also minimize the possibility of leakage at these connection points.

Holding tanks are another odor source. Be particularly suspicious of flexible waste tanks. Some early models were notorious for their permeability, and even the newer ones can chafe and leak. Also be sure the tank is vented to the outside of the boat. Aside from the smell, holding tanks give off methane gas that can build up to explosive levels.

With everything leak free, the only secret to keeping the head compart-

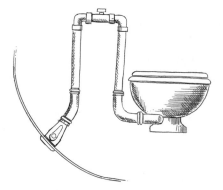

ment as fresh as a spring day is keeping it clean. That means pumping the head sufficiently after each use to clear not just the bowl but the hose as well. It also means the skipper should sit down when using the head underway, not just hope for the best. And it means a thorough disinfectant scrub of the toilet and the head compartment at least every week. It is a small price to pay.

What about overboard discharge? Away from the States it is likely your only choice because pump-out stations simply don't exist. If that offends your sensibilities, let me put your mind at ease. The small amount of fecal waste you pump overboard has no measurable ecological impact unless you are in an enclosed body of water without the benefit of tidal flushing, or unless it is combined with the discharge of hundreds of other boats in a concentrated area.

Consider this: a single blue whale digests as much as 8 tons of food every day. The waste from just one of these great mammals—excreted directly into the ocean—exceeds the combined discharge from more than 5,000 cruising sailors. While the cruising population is up, more than a century of commercial whaling has reduced the blue whale population by more than 200,000, according to conservative scientific estimates. This suggests to me that the natural cleansing capacity of the Earth's oceans has some excess capacity for the occasional wandering sailor.

This is not to recommend overboard discharge with impunity. When you are in a marina, use the shoreside facilities even though they may be less convenient, or use your holding tank and pump it out later at sea.

When you are anchored among other boats, expect that all of them are discharging directly overboard. The thought of that might leave you uncomfortable, but to allow ample swinging room, the density of anchored boats is typically low enough that water quality is essentially unaffected. Fecal coliform bacteria die off rapidly in seawater. Concentrations that might represent a health risk are virtually nonexistent away from high-volume sources like runoff or a sewer outfall.

Here is an example. The city fathers in Miami have long wanted to "clean up" a liveaboard area known simply as "the anchorage." Pollution seemed like just the unassailable justification to allow them to take action, but when the water was tested, there was no detectable difference between the quality of the water in the anchorage and the rest of the bay.

In a bit of irony, during this same period the same city had three major sewage spills from pipe or pumping station failures, each one dumping at least 5 *million* gallons of raw sewage into Biscayne Bay. Imagine commissioners directly responsible for the inadequate maintenance and safeguards that let 17 million gallons of raw sewage escape into the bay discussing the dangers of the bathroom habits of 50 or so liveaboards. That, outrageous as it is, is not why I mention these events. Rather, it is telling that just three days after a 6-million-gallon spill, fecal coliform bacteria levels were back to normal. The bay cleansed itself in less than 72 hours.

Use your holding tank when you are anchored among other boats if you like. That certainly offers aesthetic advantages if nothing else. Just be sure the tank is large enough, well-installed, nonpermeable, vented above deck, and that it has a convenient means of emptying it overboard.

It is true that some aspects of the cruising life are not as effortless as their shoreside counterparts. Unless you have very deep pockets, you are likely to sacrifice a number of conveniences. The one that will loom largest is likely to be city water—a connection to an unlimited water supply. But while you are wishing for a long shower or a washing machine, bathtubs and laundry rooms back home will be full of people dreaming of being exactly where you are. Wait until the setting sun flames the tropical sky, and frangipani scent drifts out to you from a palm-fringed crescent beach before you decide which reality you prefer.

13

Cruising with Kids

IT IS ONLY NATURAL FOR PARENTS TO BE CONCERNED ABOUT THE WELFARE OF their children. For a mother, in particular, this can be the prime source of her immunity to the lure of cruising. The main issue for her is not whether she could find fun, interest, or even reward in a cruise but whether it would be good for her children. Specific concerns are easy enough to list. Is the cruising environment safe for a child? Is it healthy? Will social skills suffer? What about education?

Raising children successfully is plenty difficult to start with, and it doesn't get easier just because you're on a boat. What does happen, however, is that fewer things compete for the time good parenting requires. It is all too easy in our society for a child to grow up without a father, even though a man named Daddy lives in the same house. The dynamic changes on a cruise, partly because Daddy doesn't go off to a job every day, and partly because— as ridiculous as it sounds—he also has a captain's responsibilities. Cruising children get to know their fathers.

Mothers have traditionally been a more constant influence in the lives of their children, but as careers have become increasingly demanding, child care has been yielded to nannies, daycare workers or, God forbid, the television. Older kids get much of their view of the world from other kids their own age—the blind leading the blind. A cruise at least temporarily releases the working mother of conflicting responsibilities. She can devote as much of her time to a child as that child requires, and she can provide that time when the child needs it.

The cruising life fosters a traditional family unit. Both parents are a constant and essential presence in a child's life, and the children participate in the family enterprise of running the boat—not unlike family life on a small farm. This is invariably good for the child and it is almost always rewarding for both parents as well.

But this is a book about cruising, not parenting, so let's get on to cruising concerns.

Safety

Are children at risk on a boat? Yes. With just a moment's inattention a small child can drown. Hot liquids—sloshing suddenly from bowls or pots—can scald. Underway the cabin is a tossing landscape of sharp angles and hard surfaces. Going outside requires ascending a steep ladder, and if that is negotiated without incident, there are plenty of opportunities on deck to get whacked, pinched, or abraded.

Life, however, is fraught with risk. Accidents are the leading cause of death of all American children regardless of age, and nearly three-quarters of those are automobile deaths—a risk cruising children rarely face. The second-leading cause of death among American children aged 10 to 19, I am sorry to repeat, is gunfire. For those under 10, it is tragically the fourth leading cause (behind birth defects and cancer). Unless *you* have a gun aboard, cruising in almost any other country in the world essentially immunizes your child from this risk.

Is this significant? I think so. Just these two cut your child's risk of death by any cause, *any cause whatsoever*, by more than half. Let me put this another way. If we ignore, for the moment, the increased risk of drowning, your child is statistically more than twice as safe cruising than at home.

As for drowning, it may surprise you that more children drown each year in buckets than off boats. The reason for this is that every parent of a child on a boat is cognizant of the risk and most take precautions, such as dressing their children in life preservers. The mother leaving her mop to answer the telephone simply doesn't recognize the danger to her toddler until too late.

Backyard swimming pools represent the greatest drowning danger. In some sunbelt states—where backyard pools proliferate—drowning is the leading cause of accidental death of children under the age of 4. Even though the water is just a quick dash away, many parents fail to think of it as a present danger. A latch that protected a toddler yesterday is ineffective today because the capability of a child at this age is changing daily. It is a tragedy that strikes nearly 600 parents every year.

Moving aboard a boat, like installing a backyard pool, increases your toddler's exposure to the risk of drowning, but the boat is actually safer for the child than the pool because *you* can't forget the risk. Once children become proficient swimmers, their risk of drowning is greatly diminished.

The first safety rule for children is the same as for parents—stay aboard the boat. Every child should have a well-fitted safety harness with which he or she can be secured when circumstances warrant. With their legendary propensity to make a sudden dash for the rail, toddlers should be tethered any time they are on deck. Older children may need their harnesses only when the boat is underway, and then perhaps only if they leave the cockpit, depending on the conditions.

Children should also have life jackets, and in the early days of a cruise you may want to make them required apparel whenever a small child comes on deck. As a practical matter, however, wearing a bulky life jacket is uncomfortable. As you get farther south, it can also be dangerously hot. Harnesses are to be preferred. Save the life jackets for trips in the dinghy and for when the weather deteriorates. They must, of course, be immediately at hand for emergency use.

A boat with small children aboard benefits from "fencing" the deck by lashing strong netting to the lifelines. Even for a harnessed child, the netting provides a second layer of protection, and it has the significant added benefit of keeping toys from going overboard. When the boat is calmly at anchor, netting allows you to let small children play unrestrained—but supervised—on the deck.

The most effective precaution against drowning is to teach your child to be comfortable in the water. Babies can learn to stay afloat before they can walk, and by the age of 3 a child can learn to be a proficient swimmer. An unexpected dunking of a child at ease with the water is less likely to result in a water-ingesting panic and more likely to result in nothing more than a funny story to tell the other kids. Most cruising children soon become amphibious, nearly as at home in the water as on land.

Drowning, of course, is not the only risk. Children can—and will—get hurt on a boat, but you can take precautions to minimize the seriousness of the injury. The usual household rules apply: make sure all medicines and chemicals are inaccessible; keep small children away from the galley stove, and

never leave pot handles turned out; and round off all pointed corners and sharp edges.

The movement of the boat makes rounded corners particularly vital and suggests a number of other precautions. The galley stove should have pot clamps to grip saucepans. There must be nothing heavy that can fall onto a child if the boat takes a deep roll off a steep wave. Even a toilet lid can be unexpectedly dangerous if it doesn't secure with a latch. Fortunately children are seldom seriously injured by falling, but there should be nothing but flat sole for your child to tumble onto at the bottom of the companionway ladder.

Watch out for motorized appliances like fans and belt-driven pumps that children can get long hair caught in. Kids are at increased risk of getting pinched by the doors and drawers in a boat, and they can injure fingers on reach-through latches. On the bright side, 12-volt outlets are infinitely less dangerous for children than the 110-volt variety at home.

Try to not be overprotective or you will take the fun out of sailing for your child. Children need to "discover" their world, and they often get bumps and bruises doing it. Of course you need to establish safe boundaries. Obedience takes on added importance on a boat. Developing a warning tone of voice early on that will stop your child in his or her tracks can be your most effective safeguard.

Small children can also put the boat at risk by opening the gas taps on the stove, but not if *you* always turn off the gas at the tank *and let the flame go out*—consuming all the gas in the line—before you turn off the burner. The solenoid switch *must* be where a child cannot get at it.

Children can flood the boat by opening the toilet valve, or damage the engine by closing a seacock. Children are drawn like a candle moth to knobs and buttons, and they can quickly damage important and expensive navigation and communications equipment, or at the very least get it out of calibration.

It is a good idea to sit down on the cabin sole to get a child's eye view. Look for features or stowage practices that represent a potential risk—either to the child or the gear—then correct them.

Most cruising hazards will be less dangerous to your child than the street that runs in front of your house. You handle them in essentially the same way—protect small children and teach older children safe behavior.

Health

It is hard for me to imagine that institutional contact with several hundred other children every school day poses fewer health risks than the relative isolation of cruising. While certain diseases may be more prevalent outside the United States, cruisers, like all tourists, are statistically at much lower risk than residents to contract endemic diseases. It is simply a matter of relative exposure.

Cruising children should have all childhood immunizations, including any required boosters. These include vaccinations for hepatitis B; diphtheria, tetanus, and pertussis (DTP); H. influenza type B; polio; and measles, mumps, and rubella (MMR). If it has been more than 10 years since your child (or anyone aboard, for that matter) has had a tetanus shot, get one prior to departure. For other health risks and possible vaccination requirements for countries on your itinerary, check with your doctor or the CDC (see health chapter).

Most popular cruising destinations present few if any additional health risks for children. Malaria is a problem in some tropical areas. The best preventative is screens on the boat and religious use of insect repellent on trips ashore. Malarial mosquitoes are nocturnal feeders, so limiting dusk to dawn visits ashore will significantly reduce the risk. Still, because children are particularly at risk for dire consequences, they should be given appropriate doses of a prophylactic drug in all malarial areas. The local health office will have up-to-date information on the type of drug to take and the appropriate dosage.

Dengue fever is also transmitted by mosquito bite. In adults the disease is usually self-limiting and benign, although benign may not seem like the right word when you are burning up, vomiting, and quite certain your head is going to explode. Dengue is not as benign in children under 15. There is no prophylactic for dengue, but fortunately the risk is small unless an epidemic is in progress. The best preventative is to avoid countries currently experiencing a dengue-fever epidemic. Screens and repellents should be adequate otherwise.

Childhood infections such as chicken pox are rare among cruising children. Colds and flus are also far less common than ashore simply because your child will have less daily intimate contact with other kids. Other types of infections are always a risk, and it would be wise to discuss with your child's pediatrician appropriate treatments for an unknown condition accompanied by high fever.

Children are also prone to skin infections. An active child is likely to have a sizable collection of cuts and scrapes, and these can quickly fester in damp tropical air. Kids also tend to scratch rashes and insect bites, fostering infection. Constantly damp feet can lead to fungal infections. Kicking barefoot down village paths sooner or later results in a staph infection.

Avoiding these infections is mostly a matter of vigilance. Disinfect every new wound. Keep kid's fingernails cut short. Let kids wear sandals or go barefoot aboard—so their feet can dry and get plenty of air—and dust fungal infections early with medicated powder. For going ashore farther than the beach, put a child's feet in enclosed shoes.

Some children are prone to ear infections, and spending hours each day in the water won't help this (although seawater is less aggravating than swimming-pool water). Water-triggered ear infections—*swimmer's ear*—can be avoided by putting a few drops of glycerol or common isopropyl alcohol (rubbing alcohol) into the ears after swimming to displace the water and dry the ear. Check with your pediatrician.

Sunburn is an ever-present risk for cruising children. A blistering sunburn in childhood has been directly related to melanoma in later life, so protect your children's skin with the same care you should be using for your own. Slip! Slop! Slap!

Head lice are not uncommon in many parts of the world, and children at play often put their heads together. Don't be dismayed if your child becomes infested. Medicated shampoos are available everywhere, but scrubbing with regular shampoo about 10 minutes a day for 10 days will usually get rid of head lice. You can remove the nits by soaking the hair for 30 minutes in a warm, half-water/half-vinegar solution, then combing thoroughly with a fine-tooth comb.

Children are just as susceptible to motion sickness as adults, and with the same degree of caprice. If your child does become seasick on the boat, the most effective cure is simply to put her or him to bed. Motion sickness tablets should not be given to children. Seasickness in children has no psychological component, so they readily admit that something is wrong, vomit if nauseated, and lie down if it makes them feel better. Most children simply go to sleep and wake up fully recovered, usually with a ravenous appetite. Oh, to have such resilience.

Like their parents, cruising children are almost invariably healthier than kids ashore. Provided they get a proper diet, the active, clean-air environment of a boat seems to help cruising kids develop a substantial resistance to infection and disease. They may exhibit a few additional nicks and bruises, but they generally have a good time getting them.

Influence

Some parents worry that breaking the continuity of a "normal" upbringing will later put their child at a disadvantage. While their child is off on a sailboat in the backwaters of the world, her peers ashore are staying current with the times and following the path that leads to well-adjusted adulthood.

Really?

Does gang graffiti deface walls and fences of the school your child attends? Are there metal detectors at the school's doors and random locker searches to try to keep weapons out? What do you suppose the ratio of drugs suppliers to career counselors is? Ten to one? Twenty to one? How much educating is really taking place, and is it teachers or other kids who seem to have the most influence on your child?

As these are the very issues that have led parents with adequate means to virtually abandon public schools, few should argue that in many American cities, removing your child from the influences of public school is likely to be a net gain. Private schools do tend to provide a safer environment and a demonstrably better education, but an inordinate number of affluent children become involved in drugs and antisocial behavior, perhaps your child among them.

School is not the only institution that influences your child, maybe not even the main one. By the time a child is 18 years old, he or she will have spent less than 14,000 hours in classrooms but between 15,000 and 20,000 hours in front of a television. That is the equivalent of watching television 24 hours a day for about 2 years. People who keep track of this assert that the average child will have viewed about 200,000 acts of violence, learned enough bad language to earn a certificate, and been inappropriately exposed to innumerable "adult" themes. I'm not going to enter into the argument about the impact of television except to ask rhetorically, if television doesn't have an impact, why do we spend billions of dollars on television advertising? If commercials have an effect, wouldn't other messages?

Regardless of how you think television influences children, too much of almost anything is bad. Cruising at least gives kids a break from television, and it demonstrates to them that real joys in life come from being a participant, not just a spectator.

A cruising child does suffer—at least early on—from the loss of playmates and friends, but except when underway, this is not the problem you may imagine. Best estimates place the number of cruising boats with children aboard at about one in three. At popular cruising destinations it is not uncommon for the beach to resemble a schoolyard playground. When one cruising family discovers another with compatible children aboard, they tend to loosely cruise in company, at least for a while, to allow the children to spend more time together.

Most kids make friends with lightning speed, and their friends aren't limited to kids from other boats. They also make quick friends ashore. Culture, language, and skin color are of no importance. When a child meets another child, it is like you or me meeting a fellow countryman in a foreign land. The world over, children are more like other children than they are like the adults of a country. They laugh at the same tricks and play nearly identical games. Since their lives are more visual than verbal, they communicate with a dexterity that adults find amazing. When words are needed, they simply teach them to each other.

Over the course of a long cruise a child will spend time with other children in a rainbow of colors, speaking a variety of languages, and exhibiting a wide array of customs. This is good for your child and good for the world. It is much easier to recognize bigotry when one of your friends is the target. And the more of the world you have seen firsthand, the harder it will be to ever have parochial views.

Cruising children are invariably more self-assured than kids ashore. Perhaps it is the living out a real adventure rather than just reading about one. Perhaps it is the direct contact with nature, "surviving" darkness, the vast ocean, or a violent storm. Perhaps self-image is boosted by standing a watch or learning to navigate. It is probably all of these and more, and it gives cruising kids confidence and independence beyond their years.

But it doesn't rob them of their childhood. The natural order of things is somehow clearer in an elemental environment. The rush to "grow up" so prevalent in shoreside society seems to get left behind when families go cruising. Kids get involved in kid things, not trying to imitate the latest fashion, sports, or entertainment idol.

Cruising provides a continual stream of fresh and varied stimuli for a fertile mind, something like a year of foreign exchange. I have yet to come across a child that didn't thrive in this environment. Children that grow up afloat or spend several years cruising do have some reintegration difficulties because they aren't "up" on the things that occupy kids ashore, like pop music, television programs, or pro sports, but this "deficiency" is soon overcome. As for children taken on a cruise of shorter duration, they invariably gain more from the experience than they lose missing a year of structured activity. For example, kids are likely to see the value of math (in my state only 15 percent of fourth graders test "proficient" in math) when they use it for navigation or to figure what their allowance is worth in a foreign port. They will better understand the value of knowing a foreign language when they need it to talk to their friends. The sciences of biology, astronomy, and physics become real and fathomable when you dive on a reef, identify constellations, and help maintain the engine. And cruising children invariable become voracious readers, a record no school can boast.

The most significant influence on cruising children, however, is their parents. I have already mentioned this, but it bears repeating. Both cruising parents have 24-hour involvement with their children, not just a couple of weeknight hours and weekends. This doesn't mean cruising children don't have separate lives. To the contrary, their lives are often fuller and more varied than the typical shoreside routine, but many activities also include the parents—if not their own, then someone's. In the cruising community there are no *paid* caregivers—an oxymoron if ever I saw one.

In the long term some children will eventually find life afloat socially limiting. In particular, the proper social development of teenagers seems to need more peer interaction than the cruising community is typically able to provide, and many families end or at least interrupt their cruise and move back ashore when a child aboard reaches 14 or 15. But this is hardly a concern for a hiatus cruise.

For me this whole issue really comes down to a single question: Do you think your influence on your own children is at least as valuable as that of the daycare or the school system or whomever they spend most of their time with now?

Education

For a long-term cruise, educating children can be a major concern, and you will need to consider a number of alternatives to select the one best for your circumstances. For the shorter term, the issue is much less complicated.

If your cruise is planned for a specific duration, say one year, and you anticipate that your child will return to the same school system, the least disruptive scheme will be for you to obtain the same books the school will use, with you filling in for the teacher. Getting a teacher's guide for each subject will make the process easier. The nearly universal appeal of sailing away can fire the imagination of a teacher or principal, and in a kind of vicarious participation they may go to great lengths to help you obtain everything you need to keep your child apace with his or her peers.

You can also simply forgo formal education for the year, letting your child learn from the life experience cruising provides. While this might actually be more "educational" than school, it is also likely to make reintegration more difficult for the child when you get home. Holding school for the duration of the cruise will ultimately be kinder.

Won't seven hours of school a day cut into the pleasures of cruising? Yes, indeed, but fortunately schooling a child requires only a fraction of that time. In the classroom environment a great deal of time is lost to distractions. And once a child among 30 understands a lesson, he or she simply waits while the teacher drills it into those still trying to comprehend. This is why bright kids often find school "boring."

To fully cover the curriculum you are unlikely to need more than an hour a day for a child under 8, two hours for one less than 12. Schooling at the secondary level typically requires about three hours a day. Most cruising parents hold school weekday mornings, leaving afternoons and weekends free. Almost all agree on the importance of a routine time schedule and regular place to study. A bulkhead reserved for posting schoolwork is also recommended.

To make the most of designated "school" hours, concentrate on the basics—reading, math, and science. Encouraging interests in music and art outside of class time can make these seem more like fun and less like learning. Similarly, if your child begins to devour books, you can spend less class time on reading, devoting that time to math or science instead.

Don't fail to take advantage of the educational opportunities cruising provides. History can become real for kids when they actually see a colonial town or sit on the barrel of a cannon. Traveling brings geography to life, and the effect is intensified by encounters with travelers from other countries. If your cruise takes you to a non-English-speaking country, your child's nimble mind will soon acquire conversational proficiency with the language. Math becomes more interesting when you show a child how to determine how far it is to shore based on bearings on charted objects, or how much water the awning will catch if it rains 1 inch. A shell collection might foster an interest in the natural sciences.

A multimedia laptop computer can provide visually interesting encyclopedias and dictionaries (without stowage problems), and you will find a

wealth of educational software that makes learning fun. If you already have a computer aboard for word processing or displaying weatherfaxes, the cost for educational software is nominal. If you are contemplating buying a computer, select one with a CD drive and sound capabilities. These add to the cost of the PC, but they are essential to get the most from educational software. Learning on the computer also improves your child's computer literacy.

Almost all children on longer cruises get their formal education through a correspondence school. These schools provide all the needed materials, including step-by-step teacher's manuals. Typically they have an associated advisory service in which a professional teacher assess work submitted by mail and provides remarks and guidance. The most well known worldwide is the Calvert School (105 Tuscany Road, Baltimore, MD 21210), but there are numerous others in the United States and other countries. Each is structured uniquely and makes varying demands on both student and teacher. Some cruising parents elect to self-develop a curriculum relevant to the stage of the cruise to supplement or even replace correspondence schooling. For a long stay in port—to wait out hurricane season, for example—cruising parents often enroll their children into the local school.

If your cruise will extend beyond a single school year, you should research the various educational options and select one—or a combination—that seems best for both you and your child. For the shorter cruise, stick with the familiar.

Infants

The boat was nearly ready. Planned departure was only three months away. Then . . . oops! They still made the trip down the Intracoastal Waterway together. The brother-in-law crewed to Nassau. There the baby was born. While Mom recovered, Dad built a thickly padded box, er, crib in the forepeak, and they were soon off again. The baby was three months old when we met them, their boat dressed in diapers cracking in the sea breeze.

Not many couples plan for their first cruising experience to include an infant, but it happens. Ironically, infants are good shipmates. They rarely suffer from motion sickness. Rather, they couldn't be happier that their whole house is a rocking chair. They sleep a large portion of every day, and as long as there is a secure crib aboard, an infant can be safely ignored when the boat demands the attention. They find endless fascination in the motion of a simple overhead mobile. And with a cloth carrier, Mom and Dad can pretty much go ashore and do most of the things they did before the baby.

The biggest problem, by far, is diapers. Enough disposable diapers to meet baby's needs for a year would completely fill a sleeping cabin on a typical cruising boat—an option not to be dismissed out of hand, because disposable diapers are quite expensive or completely unavailable in many cruising areas. Cloth diapers are the obvious answer, but keeping them clean requires a generous supply of fresh water. Most cruising parents use some combination of the two, depending on whether water or disposables are the most readily available. When the grandparents fly down for a visit, they bring the biggest duffel bag they can find, stuffed with Pampers.

Breast-feeding is especially beneficial for a cruising baby for the protection it provides against diarrhea and many infections. It also eliminates the considerable chore of sterilizing bottles and avoids many stowage problems associated with formula and bottle-feeding equipment.

Cereals and baby foods are available almost everywhere, but putting a food mill aboard will allow you to grind fresh adult foods into baby-suitable mush when (at four to six months) breast-feeding needs to be supplemented with other foods. At one year, the baby will be eating what you eat.

Babies need to be kept warm and dry when it is cool, but they need plenty of ventilation when the weather is hot. Everyone knows how sensitive a baby's skin is, but also be aware that a baby's eyes are easily damaged by too much sun. In the tropics limit on-deck time, even in the shade of an awning, to just a few minutes, and dress the infant in a wide-brimmed hat to protect the eyes.

The fact is 2 A.M. feedings and endless diaper changes are exhausting no matter where you are, but except for the absence of a washing machine, cruising doesn't particularly add to these problems—if you exclude the near-perfect acoustics inside a sailboat.

Preschoolers

Once a child is mobile, all bets are off. If this cruise is to be a "test" or a "once-in-a-lifetime" adventure, allow me to gently suggest that you not schedule it to correspond with the passage of your child through the "terrible twos." Toddlers do as well as children of other ages in the longer term, but they require so much attention to keep them safe and amused on a boat that for a six-month or one-year cruise they will detract from your ability to really explore the cruising life. Your cruise will be infinitely more enjoyable if your child is old enough not to require your full attention, and the older child will appreciate some of the wonders of cruising.

Having said this, let me also point out that children of every age can be found on boats all over the world. If your window of opportunity dictates that your cruise needs to happen while your child is a crawler or toddler, so be it. A few simple measures can make the cruise safer for the child and easier on the parents.

Start by creating a safe playpen. A bunk outfitted with bulkhead padding and fully enclosed with netting that attaches to the overhead will give you a safe place to corral the child when you are preparing a meal, answering nature's call, or needed on deck.

Speaking of on deck, a car seat adapted to the cockpit will similarly give you a convenient way to quickly immobilize the child when sailing activities require your attention. The same seat can be used for secure seating below, and you will need it anyway for inland tours you make on the cruise.

That small children love to throw things into the water is a caution worth noting, but it also means that a few colorful plastic bottles on long strings tied to the boat will keep them giggling for hours. Tow toys are also fun for toddlers when underway or anchored in a current.

At age 3 or 4, a taut line from the stern rail right through the cabin will let you tether your child so she or he has the full run of the boat—not including the side decks and foredeck. The tether should be long enough to let the child sit on the cabin sole.

Take along favorite toys and plenty of tapes and storybooks. On the plus side, Daddy can share equally in ED (entertainment duty). Another big plus is that your child isn't competing with your careers for attention. Beyond the safety of the boat, nothing else is more important than they are; it is a message that children "get."

Subteens

By the age of about 5, children no longer require constant attention. They are at the threshold of a stage in their lives when they take the world as it comes. Everything is an adventure, and life is full of exciting new capacities, like reading, or rowing, or learning to dive. Fashion, popularity, and other slave-masters are still in the future. For now the child greets each new day with wide-eyed wonder. This is without question the most favorable time to take a child cruising.

It is hard to imagine an environment that could hold more appeal for a preadolescent boy than living on a sailboat. Give him an eye patch and a wooden cutlass, and his imagination will do the rest. Little girls may not imagine themselves as Blackbeard, but most can't spend enough time in the water. Both genders are endlessly entertained by the opportunities a sailboat provides for climbing, swinging, and jumping.

The only real accommodation subteens require is their own "private" space. It is essential to have a place where a child is allowed to make a mess, and where he or she can keep toys, books, craft materials, and collections. For a single child this is usually the forward cabin. When two or more children are aboard, modifications to the boat may be needed to provide each with the needed real estate.

At this age children are often fully occupied just absorbing the world around them. When outside stimulation lags, there is plenty for them to do to ward off boredom. Swimming and diving top the list, but rowing the dinghy won't be far behind. Because of this, give strong consideration to taking a hard dinghy instead of, or in addition to, an inflatable. The hard skiff rows easier, and with a simple sailing rig, it will be as popular as a bicycle ashore. Older kids justify carrying a sailboard (and Mom and Dad are likely to enjoy it as well).

Some cruising kids of this age develop a nearly obsessive interest in fishing. Others will spend hours on the beach examining shells, dredging up sand dollars, or just poking through tideline junk. Diaries can be important, and sailing kids often develop an interest in knots and navigation. Few long avoid the lure of reading, and keeping a child supplied with books can present a substantial—and welcome—challenge.

It is important to let children this age participate in operating the boat. Even small children can be asked to call out depthsounder readings, pump the bilge, or coil lines. By 7 or 8 they can row the dinghy and take short tricks at the helm; given their own (inexpensive) binoculars, they will invariably be the first to spot navigation aids. By 10, kids can run the outboard, stand a daytime watch, and plot a course. These are the kinds of things that foster self-assurance and give children a sense of responsibility.

Teenagers

Teenagers rarely want to go cruising because they define their lives in terms of their friends, and their friends are staying behind. That doesn't mean, however, that every cruising teenager is miserable. Some succumb to the seduction of sailing, some find the laid-back life better than the pressures ashore,

and some come to see the trip as a unique adventure. Just as often, I am sorry to report, a teenager aboard hates sailing, is bored by the cruising pace, and wants nothing more than to go home.

Because cruising provides a rare and unique opportunity for parents to interact with their teenage children away from the noise of shore life, and because the child stands to gain unexpected maturity and self-confidence, and a broader view of the world, it is usually worth the effort to draw a reluctant teenager into the enterprise, particularly a child 15 or younger. When they are older than that, if they don't want to go and they are doing well ashore, you may not be doing them any favor by disrupting their lives. As with toddlers, this may be a case where you should delay the cruise until after high-school graduation. On the other hand, if you have a problem teenager, a year away from bad influences might make all the difference.

Teenagers need to be treated as equals on the boat. That means regular watches and a full share of responsibility. They also need the interaction of other teens, so you will need to always be on the lookout for other cruising families with kids of the appropriate age.

Don't overlook raging hormones at this age. A sudden infatuation can—like flipping a switch—entirely redefine a teenager's attitude about cruising. This can be a welcome change, but it may require alterations to your itinerary.

This is also the age of developing independence, and off-boat activities will be important. That may mean spending time on other boats, going diving with friends, or finding appropriate "nightlife" ashore.

Some teenagers will become voracious readers on a hiatus cruise and others won't pick up a book except in connection with schooling requirements. The longer the cruise, the more likely it is that a child aboard discovers the wonder of books. Music, however, will be important from the start, so be sure teenagers have a personal stereo with plenty of batteries aboard, and that they get the opportunity to add occasionally to their CD library. Quality of music aside, headphones provide teens with a way to be "alone"—much needed in the confines of a boat.

Teenagers are nearly adults, and their attitudes about cruising may not be that different from yours. If you want them to join you on the cruise and be happy, you will have to find a way to accommodate their needs.

The Four-Legged Variety

What do you do with your pets?

Give the goldfish away. Birds, once they get used to the motion, usually do okay. Adapting to life afloat is not quite so easy for cats and dogs.

You can immediately identify dog owners among the anchored fleet. They are the ones motoring the dinghy ashore in lashing rain to let Neptune (seagoing brother to Pluto) do his business. They go by at daybreak. They limit their own time ashore in order to get back for the dog's afternoon run. That is their outboard you hear again late at night.

The decision to take your dog cruising should not be made lightly. It will be hard enough on you having to get the animal to shore two or three times a day, but it can be much harder on the dog. Some are extremely susceptible to motion sickness, a pitiful sight indeed. Dogs also need plenty of exercise to remain healthy. If you've ever voiced doubt about the wisdom of keeping a dog in the confines of an apartment, keep in mind that a 40-foot boat has about half that space. You'll need to take the dog for a run on the beach every day, not nearly as convenient as turning him out in the backyard. Some dogs swim for exercise, but they often suffer from the salt in their fur.

Dogs are unwelcome in a number of foreign countries. Some place the dog in quarantine in a kennel *for six months,* at your expense. Others simply take the animal and destroy it. You need to check the laws of countries you might visit.

Dogs can be an effective deterrent to petty theft when you are away from the boat, but in an otherwise tranquil anchorage, if Neptune howls or yaps, he will quickly make you persona non grata.

Cats are better suited for life afloat. They are quiet. Their attitude about exercise is they can take it or leave it. They don't need to go ashore at all; a litter box is as much beach as they require. But cats do get seasick. They will relieve themselves on the upholstery when feeling peevish. They give your boat an odor that will put off many of your non-cat-owning neighbors. And surprisingly—as surefooted as cats are—they regularly fall overboard. Sometimes it's funny, sometimes not.

It is nice to be greeted by your pet every time you return to the boat. And pets are endlessly entertaining. But a dog aboard dictates the daily schedule, and cats sometimes fail to complete the voyage. Where a pet is a full family member, these issues are probably moot.

You will never find a cruising parent who thinks cruising was bad for his or her child. The experience excels in teaching self-reliance. And out of necessity children learn a respect for property absent in the throwaway society ashore. Sailing teaches kids patience and teamwork, and they form a lifetime kinship with the environment.

And it's a whale of an adventure.

14

Do You Have to Go Home?

RIGHT NOW MAYBE YOU THINK THE HAPPIEST DAY OF YOUR LIFE IS LIKELY TO be when this whole harebrained episode is over and you retie your boat in your home marina. You could be right.

But don't count on it.

Under the Spell

Let's try our hand at time travel. You are eight months into a planned one-year cruise. In a protected bay a few miles north of the Tropic of Cancer, the motion of your boat is perceptible only by the movement of shadows on deck. It is a bright April day with the temperature in the low 80s, but your mood is unexpectedly melancholy.

More than 40 other boats are anchored in the vicinity. The big ketch is new, but that is *Puff* in front of it. Joshua is rowing over to play with Jessica and Laura on *Scheherazade*. Farther out you see *Figaro*—dark under the shade of her big awning, and behind her the radical catamaran, *Starship Enterprise*. The

dinghy isn't trailing behind *Lady Blue,* so Mike and Nicki are no-doubt off diving. *Bella Donna* is festooned in towels, evidence of Donna's visiting sisters.

A splash makes you look the other way, and next to *Cool Change* you spot Robyn's blond hair in a growing circle of ripples. Beyond are *Amantes, Restless Wind, Teal, Gandalf, Princess Di, Yellowbird,* and *Scott Free.* Scott is alone, but on the other 13 boats are couples and families who have become part of your life. And there is only one degree of separation between you and all the other cruisers pausing here.

It is nearing time for you to head back, and the thoughts of separating from friends, especially Robyn and Bill and Donna and Laurent, are the source of your somber mood. The intensity of friendships you have formed has surprised you. Of course you still have friends at home, but there is somehow less time for them ashore. Here you get together regularly, combining resources for extraordinary meals, going ashore as a group, or gathering under starry skies to listen to Robyn play the guitar or Laurent spin out another of his hilarious tales.

Wait a minute!

You give your head a shake to clear it. Your family is back ashore. Friends you've had most of your life are there. You just need to reassess some of your priorities when you get back, that's all. But even if you do change, how much time will everyone else? . . .

Someone calling the name of your boat penetrates the profundity. You reach below for the microphone and respond. It is Laurent from *Bella Donna.* In the background it sounds like an aviary—Donna and her two sisters. Laurent is threatening to slash his wrists. You recommend deadly nightshade, which gets a laugh from Laurent, and Albert on *Teal* keys in to say "Good one." Linda joins the conversation, offering to pick up Laurent when she and Dan head across the harbor to "town."

With Laurent rescued, the party-line conversation turns to weather. A front and associated squall line are predicted for overnight. Here, at least, is something you won't miss—violent weather roaring over you, shaking the boat like a schnauzer with a chew toy. Although for the last couple of months you've noticed less apprehension about the weather. Maybe you're learning to trust the anchors. And anyway, back home this same front is bringing a two-day ice storm that will triple commute times and fill up body shops and emergency rooms. Here the worst will be over in a couple of hours, and behind the front the air is so clear it gives the world a gloss.

For a moment you feel content at the prospect of a good downpour because it has come to mean full water tanks and an empty hamper, then you shake your head again. At home water runs out of the spout as long as you have the faucet open—hot water, if you want it. Clean laundry is just a matter of dropping the clothes in the machine and punching a button.

This last thought annoys you. There have to be a lot stronger ties to shore than your washing machine. But you're definitely going to savor nose-level baths when you get back. Or are you? Another splash near *Cool Change* makes you suddenly aware of where you are. The beauty of the surrounding water, mottled in blending shades of turquoise and aquamarine, is still startling even after four months sailing over it. You and your partner have spent countless hours immersed in these crystal waters, gliding over waving coral teeming with iridescent fish or just floating weightlessly, suspended in both space and time. When have you ever had this kind of time to spend in the tub?

Time. It occurs to you that you aren't sure what day of the week it is. Somehow that feels impossibly luxurious compared to life ashore. No alarm clock. No schedule. It was uncomfortable at first, having to decide each day what to do, but now it feels pretty darn good being in total control of every day. You're sure your blood pressure must be lower.

You've spent a lot of that free time with a book in your hand. You haven't read so much since you used to bring stacks of library books home as a kid. Maybe it isn't just Robyn and Donna that you'll miss. In a way you will also miss E. Annie Proulx and John Irving and Bob Shacochis and Harriet Doerr, and even Donna's favorite, Dorothy Daniels.

Your sketchbook lies open on a cockpit cushion. Will you find the time to draw or paint when you get back? Will you find the inspiration? Look at this day! The water sparkles. Sand beaches gleam in the sunlight. Even the palm fronds shimmer with emerald light. At home, after day after day of winter gray, you often wondered where the sun goes. Now you know. For 100 days it hasn't failed to put in an appearance.

On the lazarette beyond the shade of the awning, the pearl interior of the conch-shell horn Nigel gave you flashes pink. It reminds you of the conch fritters, conch salad, and cracked conch you have developed a love for. Already you crave lobster, though the season has been closed for just two weeks. And after getting used to fish only an hour out of the water, you wonder if you'll ever be able to enjoy restaurant fish again?

Robyn and Bill are still in the water, sporadically snorting their snorkels clear as they brush soft growth off the bottom of *Cool Change*. It seems so natural now, being in the water. You straighten a knee and point your toes to admire the tone that has returned to your legs from a regular regimen of swimming. And walking. That, and probably the seafood diet, has flattened your tummy as well. *Lean and mean.* You grimace at how that sounds. You feel good, anyway. You can admit to that.

Little Laura's squeal draws your attention to the beach. Sandpipers scurry in front of her in a blur of stick legs, but as soon as she turns around, they follow her like a trailing brood of ducklings. Your smile makes you realize how much pleasure you have found in unexpected quarters—rainbows and moonrises and finding bird peppers in the market. Thoreau said it: "Simplify. Simplify. Simplify." Life is less complicated here. *That* you will miss—more and more, you are sure, as your life ashore spins faster and faster.

And then there are just the plain bad things back home. A job you don't enjoy. Traffic. Smog. Noise. Hay fever. Bills. Debt. And the nightly news trifecta—crime, violence, and corruption.

You could decide it's a big price to pay for long showers and air conditioning.

Beyond the Horizon

There is another allure of cruising that might snare you. Ashore our quest is typically prosperity. On the boat it becomes exploration. A new place to discover is always only a few miles away. "We are this close," the argument goes, "so it would be a shame not to at least go there." "There" has a picturesque setting, a notable eatery, an interesting natural wonder, an abundance of sea life, or some other attraction.

One of the worst things about life ashore can be the sameness of it. Life falls into a pattern that is repeated day after day. Cruising has no such routine. Each new day is a day of discovery. Who will sail into the anchorage? What will the weather bring? What new vegetable is offered in the market? What arts and crafts are practiced here? What treasure will you find washed up on the beach? With what new author will you find resonance? Will you like the taste of sapodilla?

And when the novelty of one place begins to wane, the promise of fresh experiences is always just over the horizon. That some of your friends are probably already there adds the appeal of reunion. It is a combination that can be hard to resist.

Twenty Years to Life

What if—just what if—you get to the turn-around point of your planned itinerary and discover you aren't that excited about heading back? Cruising has turned out to be exciting and fun and far more fulfilling than you expected. You take special pleasure in the freedom, the climate, the community, the potential in each new day. In an irony not lost on you, life afloat, even without all the comforts of home, turns out to be easier than life ashore. And from this distance, what you were doing ashore no longer seems all that important.

Whether this change of heart puts you in a quandary depends on whether the carriage turns back into a pumpkin at midnight.

Most first cruises conclude more or less on schedule. The house has been leased for a year. A hard-won sabbatical requires your return on a specific day. Your business can only run so long without your oversight. You didn't plan for the kids to be away from formal schooling more than a year. Maybe your account balances are dwindling. Or you just don't want a missing calendar year on your résumé.

But the desire to continue cruising is common enough to look at how it can be accommodated. The most common course is to return as planned, beginning almost immediately to work toward returning to the cruising life. This might involve selling a house and/or a business, buying a different boat, or beginning a major savings program. The target departure date might be less than a year away or more than five. Worthy of note is that for the enthusiastic cruiser, one of cruising's best pleasures can be the preparation.

When the ties with shore are more tenuous, you might be able to fly home for a few weeks and make all the additional arrangements required to at least extend the length of your cruise. This could be little more than visiting family and making a few banking and investment decisions, or it could mean submitting a resignation and listing a home for sale. Flying home has the advantage of leaving the boat where it is, but if you are making wholesale changes in your lives, urgency can be a disadvantage.

A more flexible arrangement is to put the boat in dry storage before you fly home. This removes any real urgency to return, allowing you to focus on making your best decisions at home regardless of how long some issues may take to resolve advantageously. Keep in mind that not sailing home adds weeks or months to your outward track, allowing you to select a storage location well beyond your anticipated terminus. This can be especially significant for hurricane season.

Some bitten by the cruising bug don't give up life ashore but rather structure their shore lives to allow a few weeks or months each year for cruising. They pick up their boat at point A and cruise for the allotted time to point B. The following year they pick up the boat from point B and sail to point C, and so on. This works particularly well for seasonal and faraway cruising such as gunkholing in the Baltic or exploring northern Europe.

How long can a cruise last? For a few people it becomes a permanent lifestyle, but for most others it is no more than a passage leading to the rest of their lives. Along the way they discover what they want to do next, or they find where they want to live. Doesn't examining your life and sampling the world make better sense than clinging to career decisions made as a child or letting an employer dictate where you live?

For some the cruise becomes self-sustaining. They are content to follow an seemingly aimless track, moving on when the mood strikes. When they find a place they particularly like, they pause weeks or months—sometimes years—to sample all it has to offer.

Others need to redefine the goal of the cruise. The original plan of taking a year off to sail to the Caribbean and back gives way to destinations farther afield—French Polynesia or perhaps the Greek Isles. Some set their sights on the whole enchilada—circling the globe.

Goals can pull a cruise through the inevitable thorny patch, but they can also keep a crew cruising when everyone would be happier if the cruise were over. I take a hedonistic view: do it as long as it seems like there is fun still ahead.

Voyaging

It is easy enough to cruise extensively without ever spending a night under-way. Even a cruise to Baja or through the islands of the Caribbean will necessitate only the occasional overnight passage. But if you're game to spend a few days at sea, the whole world is within your reach.

Consider Europe, for example. At the modest average speed of 5 knots, Bermuda is less than six days—five nights—from the eastern seaboard of the United States. Bermuda is a worthy destination alone, but it is also the first stepping stone in an Atlantic crossing. The passage from Bermuda to the Azores should take about two weeks. Like Bermuda, the Azores are a spectacular cruising destination, and you will want to pause there for a while. Portugal, the next step, is only a week away.

If you have visited Europe in recent years, you know how expensive hotels and restaurants are in almost all countries, a trend that is likely to continue as the EEC draws closer together. With only two continuous weeks at sea, and two less significant passages, you now have a home in Europe. You don't need a hotel room and don't have to take every meal in a restaurant. With only a modest budget you can spend as much time as you like exploring

all of Europe, including taking your home/boat into the extensive and fascinating canal system that crisscrosses the continent.

If your interest lies west, in the far islands of the Pacific, your longest
passage will be close to three weeks. If that seems unimaginable, you should
know that just like ashore, one day follows another on a passage. Sooner than
you expect, your destination appears as a smudge on the horizon, then grows
to land of impossible height and breathtaking green. Suddenly your anchor
is down, the boat is still, and you can't believe the voyage is behind you.

What is voyaging like? With just two aboard, it is mostly tiring. Four
hours on and four off day after day wears on you. In good weather, six-hour
watches can be more restful.

Steering today is handled mostly by a vane or an electric autopilot, but
it is not unusual for voyagers to report that they went for several days without
adjusting the sails. With nothing to do but keep watch and keep track of where
you are, a voyage can also be boring. You will do a lot of reading, listen to a lot

of music, or endear yourself to your partner with creative time in the galley.

Voyaging can also be frightening. The big unknown of any voyage is the weather. On short passages you can pick your weather, but on a voyage you take what you get. The best you can do is make your passage during the most favorable time of year, but if you have ever seen a long-planned outdoor wedding rained out in June, you know how fickle the weather can be. Still, many cruisers sail for years without ever encountering sustained winds at sea heavier than a strong breeze—about 25 knots. Most low-latitude voyages suffer from too little wind, not too much. If this falls short of the reassurance you need, keep in mind that a well-found cruising boat snugged down and buttoned up is up to any sea conditions you might encounter on a wisely planned voyage.

Above all, a voyage is satisfying. When it is over, you have accomplished something that even today is still a relatively unique feat. It leaves you with a powerful sense of self-confidence, and it will make others view you with new respect. And there is no thrill on the planet quite like seeing your destination appear on the bow after days at sea. There is only one way to truly know what that is like.

Whether your cruise ends as planned or continues on to more distant horizons, it will lift you above the mundane. When the late Paul Tsongas decided not to seek reelection to the Senate on learning he had lymphoma, he said, "No one on their death bed ever says, 'I wish I had spent more time in the office.'" It is an observation worth contemplating.

Cast your reluctance aside and take a little time out to explore the world around you. Who knows what you might discover.

Index

accommodations: for babies, 163–64; bunks and bedding, 59–60, 65, 66; cabin lighting, 11, 42–43; for children, 40, 165, 166; comfort, 24–25, 38; decoration, 43–44; fabrics, 44; for guests, 40, 59–60; head, 150–52; insect screens, 115; layout, 39; pillows, 25, 42, 66; privacy, 40; rounded corners/safety precautions, 36, 93, 115, 155–56; seating, 25, 42, 44; ventilation/fans, 11, 40–42, 115–16
see also galley

activities and entertainment, 2–3, 11, 25, 172, 173; books and reading, 25, 167; for children, 165, 166, 167–68, 172; music and CDs, 3, 11, 167–68

awnings: for drying sheets, 149; for rain catchment, 8, 48, 142–43; for sun protection, 136–38

bartering, 146
bilge pump, 98
bills, paying, 105
boat: dry storage/returning to, 174; maintenance, 36; safety, 35–36, 95

boathandling and navigation: anchoring, 36, 91–92; basics, 82–94; for children, 166; compass course, 85; docking, 87–89; GPS, 93; handling the boat alone, 27, 32, 34–35, 83; knots and lines, 87–90; powering, 83–84; sailing, 85–87; sailing terminology, 93–94; sea legs, 92–93; steering, 83–84, 85, 176–77; watches, 176

cancer: breast, 138–39; colon, 138–39; skin, 129–32, 133
canvas: for awnings, 137; pockets, 65–66; shelves, 65, 66
captain: authority and style, 29–32; father as, 153, 161, 162, 166; rights and responsibility, 29–32, 33, 36–38; seamanship skills, 36–37

children, cruising with, 153–68; accommodations, 40; boathandling and navigation, 166; education, 161–63; friends/influence, 159–61, 167; health, 157–59; infants, 155, 163–64; parent-child relationships, 24, 40, 153–54, 161, 166–68; safety, 154–57; subteens, 155, 165–66; teenagers, 155, 166–68; toddlers and preschoolers, 155, 164–65

chlorine bleach, for sterilizing fruits and vegetables, 71–73

cleaning, 34; galley, 125–26; housekeeping, 149–50; sanitation/head, 150–52

clothing, 6, 10, 55–57, 103; insulating layers, 55, 56; footwear, 56–57, 59, 97, 115; foulweather gear, 55, 57–59, 96, 97; hats, 13, 133–34; for hot climates, 55–57; laundering, 10, 55, 146–49; local customs, 6, 55, 57; stowage, 64–65; for sun protection, 13, 56, 133–35

cockpit dodger, 138

communications, 104–13; beepers, 111; cell phones, 111–12; distress calls, 99–100; ham radio, 109–11, 113; mail, 105; satellite telephones, 112–13; SSB radio, 99, 108–9, 110, 113; VHF radio, 36, 99–100, 103, 105–8, 109, 110, 113

cooking, *see* galley; provisions

cookware, 61–62; pressure cooker, 61–62, 126; pump thermos, 48; stowage, 63

couples, cruising: boathandling and navigation basics, 82–94; captain's rights and responsibility, 29–32, 33, 36–38; division of labor, 12, 33–35, 54; getting along in close quarters, 12–13, 23–24, 40; mate's rights and responsibility, 28, 30–38, 54, 83; power and equality, 23–24, 28–38

cruising: as permanent lifestyle, 33, 174–75; as sabbatical, 25–26, 32, 170–73, 174–75; voyaging, 175–77

cruising destinations, 2, 5–7, 32–33, 175–76; Azores and Portugal, 6, 175; Bahamas and Caribbean, 6, 18, 49, 175; Baja coast, 6, 175; Bermuda, 175; Europe, 6–7, 175–76; Galápagos, 6, 18; Panama and Central America, 6, 18; South Pacific and Polynesia, 6, 18, 176

cruising life, benefits, 1–7, 170–77; emancipation from schedule, 2–3, 6–7, 25, 171–72; family life, 24; friendships, 3–5, 17–19, 25, 113, 170–71, 173; health and well-being, 21–23, 114–16, 124, 128, 138–39, 159, 172; stress reduction, 23, 116, 172; travel/exploration, 5–7, 175–77

cruising life, risks and concerns, 14–21, 26–27,

95, 114; boredom, 25; for children, 154–57; collisions/sinking, 15, 95, 99, 98, 103; close quarters, 12–13, 23–24; crime/assault, 19–20; discomfort/inconvenience, 8–12, 24–25, 38, 172, 173; dropping out, 25–26; drowning, 95, 154–55; family/staying in touch, 104, 113; fire/burns, 49–51, 98, 154, 155–56; flooding, 98, 157; forces of nature, 20–21; illness/infection/poisoning, 115, 117, 122–26, 157–58, 164; injury, 85, 95, 97, 115–17, 124, 154, 155–56; man-overboard, 27, 36, 37, 83, 85, 96–97; political unrest, 38; seasickness, 92, 159, 164; skin cancer, 13, 129–32; storms, 7–8, 16, 37–38, 171, 177

decks, nonskid, 35; deck shoes, 56–57, 97, 115
dishes, 61–62; glassware and jars, 61, 76; mugs, 61; stowage, 63; utensils, 61
dishwashing, 12, 34, 47, 142

electrical system: appliances, 10–12, 51–53; energy conservation, 10–11; power requirements, 10–12, 47, 51
emergencies, 14–23, 26–27, 83, 85; abandoning ship, 99, 102–3; determining position in, 93; distress calls, 99–100, 113; fire, 98; flooding, 98, 157; getting help, 17–19, 36, 99–100, 114, 117; injury/first aid, 85, 97, 115–17, 124; man-overboard, 27, 36, 37, 83, 85, 96–97; medical/illness, 14–15, 21–23, 83, 100, 114, 115, 117, 124–27; sinking, 98, 99, 103; signaling in, 100–102
see also cruising life, risks and concerns
eyes: prescription lenses, 128; sun damage/protection, 132–33, 164

family: communication with, 104, 110, 111, 113; cruising experience, 24, 40, 153–54, 159–63, 166–68
fishing, 79–80, 103, 124–25, 166, 172
food, *see* provisions
food poisoning, 124–25; botulism, 125; ciguatera, 124–25; \I\E. coli\R\, 126; salmonella, 125–26
footwear, 56–57; deck shoes, 56–57, 97, 115; leather/mildew, 57; seaboots, 59
foulweather gear, 55, 57–59; rainsuit, 58–59
friendships, 26, 171; for cruising children, 159–61; communications, 104, 110, 113; cruising community, 3–5, 17–19, 25, 113, 170–71, 173

galley, 41, 44–53; cooking, 12, 34, 47, 97; cooking techniques, 49–51, 61–62, 126,

142; cookware, 48, 61–62, 63, 126; counters, 45, 125; cutting boards, 103, 125; design/layout, 45; dishes, 61–62, 63; dishwashing, 12, 34, 47, 142; garbage, 46; refrigeration, 11–12, 51–53, 71, 73, 75, 126; safety precautions, 45, 49–51, 97, 155–57; sanitation, 125–26; sinks, 45–46, 47; stoves, 49–51, 98, 115, 155–57; stowage, 63, 64, 66, 71–74, 76, 80, 81; water supply, 46–49, 142
see also provisions
guests, bunks and bedding for, 40, 59–60

hair: haircuts/coiffure, 146; sun protection, 136; washing and conditioning, 145
head (marine toilet): cleaning and deodorizing, 150–52; pumping/discharging, 151–52
health and first aid, 114–28; for children, 157–59; doctors/health care, 114–15, 117, 126–27; exercise, 22–23; first aid kit, 103, 114, 118–22, 155; head lice, 158; health benefits of cruising, 21–23, 114–16, 124, 128, 138–39, 159, 172; health insurance, 127–28; illnesses and infections, 115, 117, 122–24, 126, 157–58, 164; injuries, 85, 95, 97, 115–17, 124, 154, 155–56; medical library, 117–18; poisoning, 124–26; prescription drugs, 120–22; prescription lenses, 128; seasickness, 92, 159, 164; sunburn, 158; windburn, 138; vaccinations, 123–34, 157
see also sun protection

insects: diseases and illnesses transmitted by, 122; roaches, 71; screens, 115
insurance, health, 127–28

laundry, 34, 146–49; clothing, 10, 55, 146–49; diapers, 164; hamper, 149; handwashing onboard, 10, 147–48; laundromats, 147; linens, 147, 148, 149; soaps/detergents, 148; towels, 60, 148, 149; water supply for, 8–9, 147, 164, 171–72
life jackets, *see* safety/survival equipment
life rafts, *see* safety/survival equipment
linens and bedding: laundering, 147, 148, 149; sheets, 59–60, 65, 147, 148, 149; stowage, 65, 66

maintenance, 36
marinas, 32, 41, 140, 141, 147
mate: boathandling and navigation basics, 82–94; handling the boat alone, 27, 32,